PLAY
ALL THE WAY

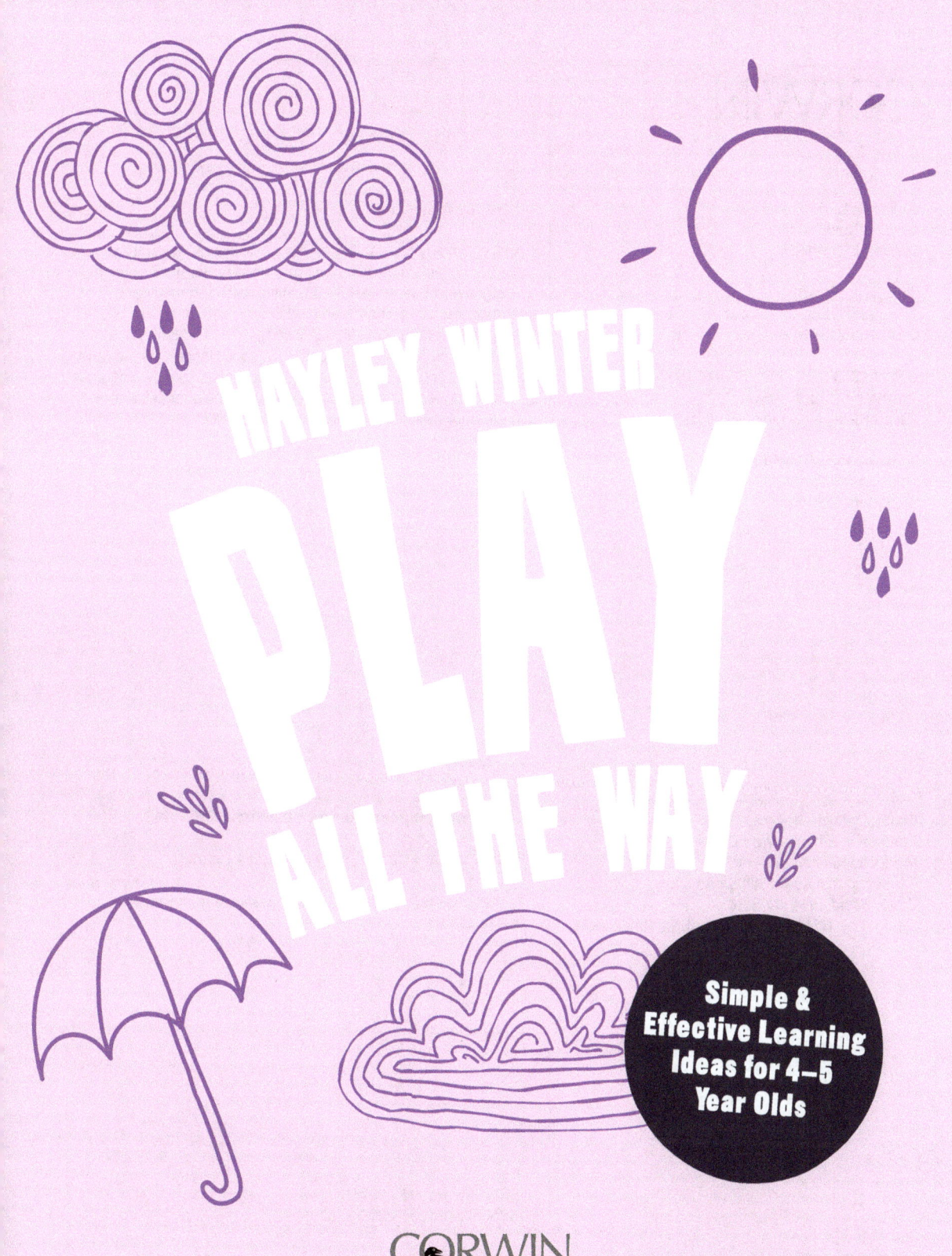

HAYLEY WINTER

PLAY
ALL THE WAY

Simple & Effective Learning Ideas for 4–5 Year Olds

CORWIN

A SAGE Publishing Company

1 Oliver's Yard
55 City Road
London EC1Y 1SP

2455 Teller Road
Thousand Oaks,
California 91320

Unit No 323-333, Third Floor, F-Block
International Trade Tower
Nehru Place, New Delhi – 110 019

8 Marina View Suite 43-053
Asia Square Tower 1
Singapore 018960

Editor: Delayna Spencer
Editorial assistant: Harry Dixon
Production editor: Ian Antcliff
Marketing manager: Dilhara Attygalle
Cover design: Wendy Scott
Typeset by: C&M Digitals (P) Ltd, Chennai, India

Library of Congress Control Number: 2023951490

British Library Cataloguing in Publication data

A catalogue record for this book is available from the British Library

ISBN 978-1-5296-2207-2
ISBN 978-1-5296-2206-5 (pbk)

Contents

Activities

Welcome!

Firstly, let's just get it out of the way shall we ... you are amazing! The work you do (whether that's as a parent, teacher, nursery nurse or both) with children is the most important in this stage between birth–5 years old.

Never forget the impact **YOU** *have during this time.*

Next, let's remember every teacher has their own pedagogy throughout their career and this can change and develop. In addition to this, every school is different. We don't have the same demographic, the same staffing structure etc, so please take this book as your initial starting point and then develop what works for your own school/cohort.

My journey

Now, let's get into a little bit about me. Although I am currently an Early Years Teacher and Lead (of my school and recently trust too) I have had many roles within the Early Years sector. I'll never forget the day I went for my first full time nursery nurse job and I didnt get it because, 'you're too qualified, you've got lots of GCSEs and A levels, go to uni or something with your education'. Let's just say that didn't go down well with me. Just because I was able to be successful at school, doesn't mean I wanted to continue in education myself, or agreed with the lack of value for the people the nursery worked with and employed. This clearly wasn't the nursery for me anyway. But this didn't deter me; the right nursery was out there for me, and this still sticks with me today. It is so important to ensure you find 'your setting', whether that's a nursery, school or workplace. I believe you just get that feeling, the sense of belonging, feeling valued and welcomed. But let's get back on track with my journey ... I found my nursery and I loved it! I've been in every age group and I originally thought I'd found my age group in the nursery (1 ½–2 ½ year-olds). That was before one day going into nursery and being told I needed to lead the pre-school group that day and from then on. But turns out this is where my passion and thoughts of becoming a teacher started. So from babies to toddlers to preschool, I've been a nursery nurse within a private nursery and day nursery.

However, once I decided to become a teacher (at 24 years old) my nursery wasn't supportive of releasing me for one day a week to complete my studies. So, on went the search for a nursery who would. Completing my degree one day a week while working 8am–6pm was hard, there's no denying that, but through determination and my stubbornness it was all worthwhile and, even more than that, my experience in nurseries and within early education has made me an even better teacher to this day.

Within the second year of my degree, it was time for a new challenge and to learn more about school life. I found it so hard to be turned away from so many jobs because I still needed my day release, but finally I found a local school who would accept me working four days as a 1:1 teaching assistant. Everything I learnt here was about valuing teaching assistance and opened my eyes to supporting all learners neurotypical or neurodiverse. I have taken so many of these lessons into my job today.

The third year of my degree brought me to another exciting opportunity. A brand new school opened up in my city (still my school today). The nursery needed a person with an NVQ level 3 qualification and they were willing to see my potential in becoming a teacher. Yet again, so many lessons learnt along the way, and starting at a brand new school allowed me to have an impact on what it looked like, secure the resources we needed with no budget, and even see it as a construction site. This is where I gained further experience in schools as a teaching assistant in Year 2, but we all know Early Years has my heart! I passed my degree in Early Childhood Studies with a First and I am so proud of myself for that.

Applying for my teacher training course (SCITT– School Centred Initial Teacher Training), I was very lucky to be given a salaried placement at a school within my trust. However, upon taking the English test to be able to start my training, I had a problem. I had to pass within three attempts, or I couldn't start the SCITT for another three years at least ... I had failed twice. Time to get a tutor. During my time within my weekly sessions, my tutor asked me if I had ever been tested for dyslexia. (Who makes a word spelt like this for someone who can't spell I'll never know!) I hadn't, but after discussion with him (he supported dyslexia assessments as his day job) he was almost certain I was dyslexic. For me, this helped me come to a realisation that while I had always thought I just didn't like English at school and couldn't spell, in reality I had built strategies for myself to cope. I would not use certain words and rearrange a whole sentence just to not use that word. I realised that the dread I felt when I had to read aloud in class was all for a reason. I cried when I passed my English test on my third attempt. All that hard work of completing my degree whilst working full time, the sacrifices I had made along the way, it was all worth it. And after all this even writing this book!

My teacher training was great; this was where I learnt you have to be your own cheerleader. I say to my team now, people forget to tell you how amazing you are so it's about time we start to tell ourselves. This is also where I met my incredible teacher bestie, Katie. Some of you will know her from when I finally persuaded her to join social media as @katiesclassroom_. Our friendship blossomed week by week and I'm so thankful I have that person to be a cheerleader, rant to and go through our teaching journey of ups and downs together with. Funny story about how we first met (although she'll deny it!): First day at teacher training, I was signing in on the school system and she comes up to me, taps me on the shoulder and asks me 'Are you Hayley?' Obviously I said 'yes' in a confused way because she was a complete stranger to me. Katie replies 'I thought so. My deputy said a ginger was going to be training in Foundation at my school and I thought it must be you.' It didn't bother me and I thought it was great to know someone who was going to be in the same school as me! We laugh about it now because this is something Katie wouldn't usually say, but I won't ever let her forget the story. I appreciate our friendship so much. I was bridesmaid at her wedding and we're starting up a club together to support other teachers in EYFS and KS1. Get yourself a teacher bestie! We have even started a business together called 'The Powerful Play Teachers' so come check us out.

From taking over as EYFS Lead just before COVID-19 and leading the team through those tough times, to building an incredible team and supporting their confidence and development in our little ones' lives, and now taking on my new role as EYFS Trust lead ... Early Years will always have my heart.

It's crazy to me that I started moving my photos to an Instagram account just as another way of storing them and now I am sharing my teaching journey and building a fabulous supportive community. I will be eternally grateful for all of you in this community. I always think 'this is just little old me, sharing what I do, day in and day out, the ups and the downs, the realities of teaching'. Yet I have been given so many opportunities, such as this one to write my own book. Dyslexic me, writing a book! 🤯

Now, here it is. The hours, days, weeks and months going into this, is like nothing before. I love Early Years because you can be flexible and creative with your curriculum and you see the huge progress the children make before your very eyes. Yes, it's undervalued, yes it's under funded and yes it's really hard work, but it's magical!

How to use this book

This book is meant to be used as a starting point to spark an idea from, when you just get that planning session where you have a mind blank. This book is full of activity ideas for the seven areas of learning (colour coded per area of learning, because clearly that's how my brain works).

First and foremost, the most important factor of this book is a **clear warning**. This is not a tick list. You shouldn't think, if my child/ class completes these activities they have met the learning objective or Early Learning Goal (ELG). This is not a guide to interact with children. This is not an assessment criteria outline. This is not how this book should be used.

As we know, children can take learning in many different ways and the ideas within this book are to be taken as a **starting point to engage children in igniting their curiosity to play**. These ideas are to be adopted as needed to different cohorts and children, and this does not mean a child has achieved the learning objective. Children should be encouraged to experiment and explore within the ideas so that if they don't do exactly what the book says they still have a rewarding experience. The very definition of play is that it is freely chosen and intrinsically motivated and this must be clear otherwise less experienced practitioners may undermine the fun and joy of the activities by being too prescriptive.

In addition, children learn and develop at their own rates. Although these activities are based on the reception-aged children's learning intentions from *Development Matters* (Department for Education, 2023a) these activities can be adapted to suit an individual child. If you have any concerns for your child's development, please speak to their class teacher or your local GP.

'While there is a statutory duty that providers must help children work towards the ELGs, the government has stated that the ELGs themselves are NOT the curriculum. Settings can determine what, when and how to offer experiences and support to help children make progress in their learning and development from birth to five.' *Birth to Five Matters* (Early Years Coalition, 2021: 7).

Early Years Framework

The Early Years Foundation Stage (EYFS) sets standards (from the government) for the learning, development and care of children from birth to 5 years old in England.

There are two different types of framework: statutory and non-statutory.

The Early Years Framework is statutory, issued by law (updated in 2024) and used by school leaders and staff, childcare providers, childminders and out-of-school providers, although there is now a separate framework for group and school-based providers and the childminders. 'The EYFS sets the standards that all early years providers must meet to ensure that children learn and develop well and are kept safe. It promotes teaching and learning to ensure children's "school readiness" and gives children the right foundation for good future progress through school and life'. (DfE, 2024: 7).

In simple terms, this framework is here to ensure ALL children have access to education and are kept safe. Within this framework, there is guidance on learning and development requirements, assessment, safeguarding and welfare. This is a must read for any individual working with children from birth to 5 years old.

Development Matters (updated in 2023), and *Birth to Five Matters* (revised in 2021) are non-statutory guidance for EYFS. This means settings do not have to follow or use this guidance. Both guides are to be used as support documents to help build an effective curriculum, but do not replace professional judgement.

> ***Curriculum = everything you want children to experience, learn and be able to do.***

Development Matters and Birth to Five Matters both use broad ages and stages because, as we know, children's learning is not linear, neat and orderly. Both guides are NOT designed to be used as a tick list for generating lots of data.

Areas of learning and development

There are seven areas of learning and development which shape the educational programmes/your curriculum, and are all inter-linked. Although they are all interlinked, they are split into two sub areas: prime and specific.

The prime areas of learning are:

- Personal, Social and Emotional development
- Communication and language
- Physical development.

'These areas are particularly important for building a foundation for igniting children's curiosity and enthusiasm for learning, forming relationships and thriving (DfE 2024: 8).

Think of these as your **foundations** for learning.

The specific areas of learning are:

- Literacy
- Mathematics
- Understanding the world
- Expressive arts and design.

These are the areas 'through which the three prime areas are strengthened and applied' (DfE, 2024).
Think of these as your **building blocks** for learning.

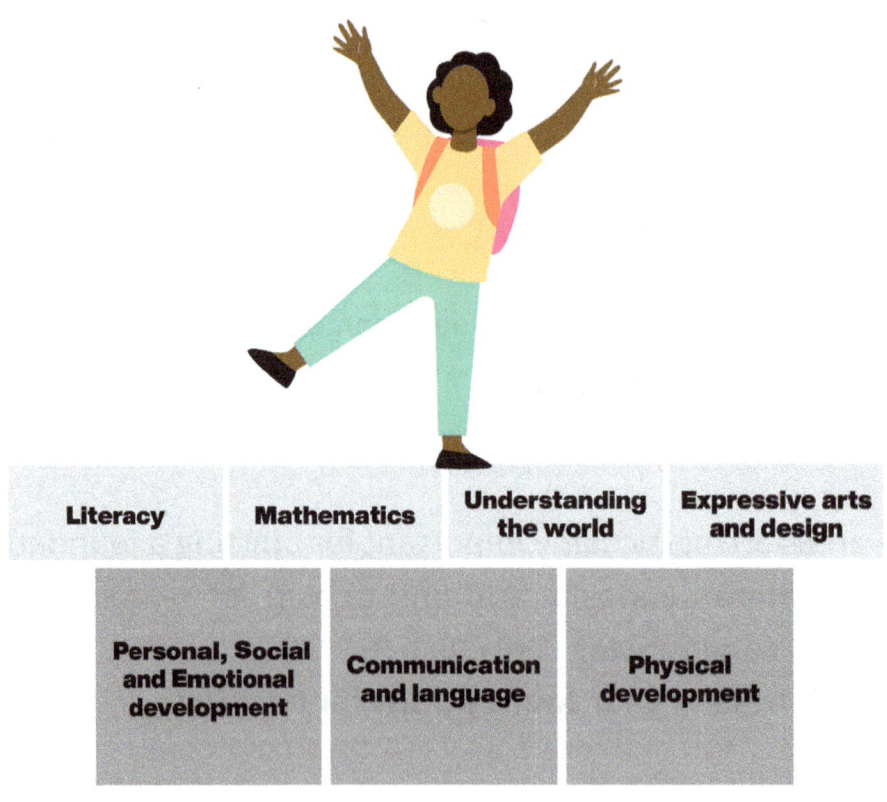

EYFS principles

The EYFS statutory framework has four principles which underpin all the non-statutory guidance. These are: a unique child; positive relationships; enabling environments; and learning and development. How a child receives these four principles will determine how their learning and development progresses because a child's experience during their early years strongly influences a child's future development. For example, if a child is able to form positive relationships within a stable home life, they are much more likely to be able to be actively ready to learn, unlike an individual who cannot form relationships. Consider Maslow's hierarchy of needs; we all need our basic needs met before we are able to develop the higher levels.

The EYFS statutory framework states these principles should shape practice within the Early Years:

- Every child is a **unique child**, who is constantly learning and who can be resilient, capable, confident and self-assured

- Children learn to be strong and independent through **positive relationships**

- Children learn and develop well in **enabling environments** with teaching and support from adults, who respond to their individual interests and needs and help them to build their learning over time

- Importance of **learning and development**. Children develop and learn at different rates.

(DfE, 2024: 7)

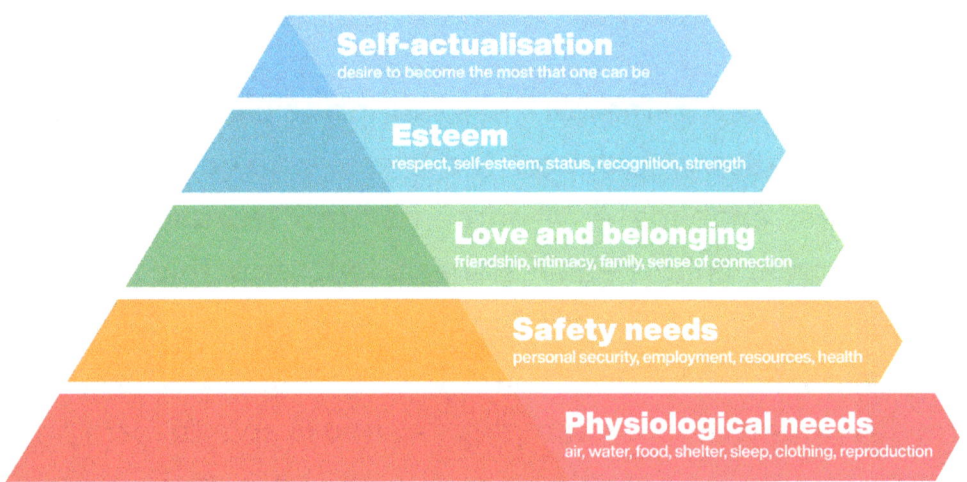

So if you're anything like me, you'll be thinking by now ... what impact does all this statutory and non-statutory guidance have in my real life settings? Well of course, if you haven't got an outside area, no one is expecting you to go knocking down houses to make one, or bringing out all the bells and whistles to make your enabling environment more natural and magically gain more staff (although we'd all love that!). It's about working with what you do have. Understanding where your setting families are from, their backgrounds, and how you can work together for the best interest of the child (because at the end of the day, that's what we're here for). Supporting your practitioner knowledge about each individual and the Early Years framework to understand what individual support the child may need next. Using what already exists to create a welcoming, calm and inclusive environment. And most of all, working collaboratively with other practitioners and parents/carers to support each individual child to become a success.

Characteristics of effective teaching and learning

The seven areas of learning and development and the four principles of the EYFS statutory framework are all interconnected once more in supporting practitioners in developing a child's learning. I know, so much to remember and so many connections and interlinked parts ... Early Years are complicated, right?

Simply, the characteristics of effective teaching and learning describe the behaviours children use to learn.

There are three:

- **playing and exploring** – children investigate and experience things, and 'have a go'

- **active learning** – children concentrate and keep on trying if they encounter difficulties, and enjoy achievements

- **creating and thinking critically** – children have and develop their own ideas, make links between ideas, and develop strategies for doing things.

(DfE 2024: 17)

Effective learning must be meaningful to a child, so that they are able to use what they have learned and apply it in new situations. For example, if they have learnt to count but never seen coins, how will they know what 5p looks like? We need to be able to expose children to hands-on learning opportunities to create a wide range of knowledge and understanding for the child to link together to be able to practise and apply these skills.

Play and set-ups

Firstly, children's right to play is recognised as so vital to their wellbeing and development that it is included in *The United Nations Convention on the Rights of the Child* (UNICEF, 1989: page 10, Article 31). The most frustrating thing about being an Early Years teacher is that often this is refered to as 'just play'. Everyone needs to realise playing is learning, playing is practising skills, playing is so much more than 'just play'.

One of the best ways for children to learn is through hands-on experiences, which is why it is fundamental to allow children to play both inside and outside. Children learn through exploring their environment and building confidence as they do this, relating to others, setting their own goals and solving problems along the way. Children learn by leading their own play and by taking part in play which is guided by adults. Children need adults to 'scaffold' their learning by giving them just enough help to achieve something they could not do independently (DfE, 2024).

PLAYING IS ...

Exploring Talking Thinking Imagining Inventing Risk taking

Sharing Making choices Challenging Turn-taking

Making friends Being yourself Roleplaying Negotiating

Performing Counting Reading Developing language

Connecting Rehearsing Writing Measuring

Trying things out Leading Following Problem-solving

Storytelling Building Laughing Smiling

Playing is learning!

Play gives a child an opportunity to practise what they've been taught.

What is provision?

There are multiple types of provision. Think of this as a triangle; at the bottom you have continuous provision, in the next layer you have enhanced provision, and finally at the top you have adult led.

Continuous provision is the resources which are always there and that children can access freely. They should be familiar to the children and enable a child to revisit and build on prior learning, with or without

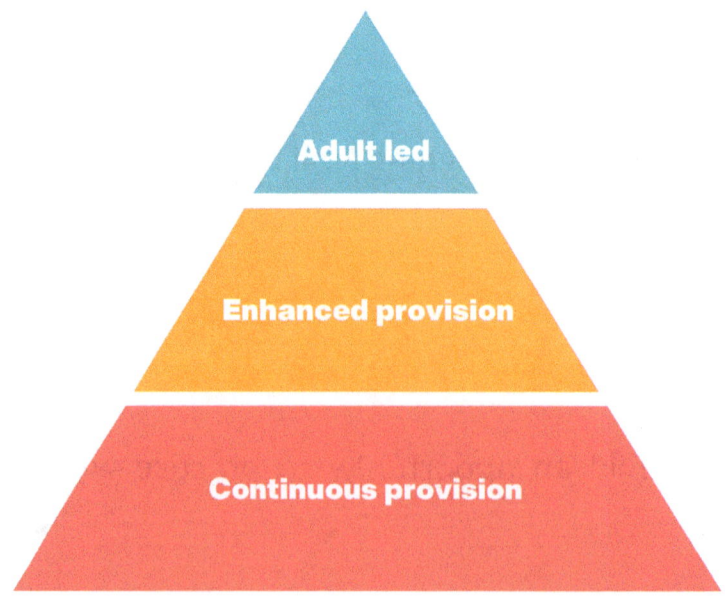

an adult. Imagine your local supermarket: you walk in and you know exactly where to find the bread. This is what continuous provision is like for children. I want to play with the dressing up, I know exactly where to go to find it. These resources never change and are a constant for the children.

Enhanced provision is anything you have added to the continuous provision to enhance it; this is usually linked to a topic. For example, if you are learning about the three billy goats gruff and added pictures of bridges to the construction area.

Adult led is where adults have planned and provided opportunities for children to be introduced to or further develop skills and knowledge which has a set outcome.

There is so much more to say about play but I really could go on and on, so I'll save that for another time.

Learning objectives and ELGs

At the end of the year, children are assessed against the Early Learning Goals (ELGs) in each of the areas of learning. Teachers will assess them to check if they have met the expected level of development or are emerging in this area. To reach a good level of development, children need to have reached the ELG in each of the prime areas of learning as well as literacy and mathematics.

As stated in the EYFS framework, 2024:

The ELGs should not be used as a curriculum or in any way to limit the wide variety of rich experiences that are crucial to child development, from being read to frequently to playing with friends. Instead, the ELGs should support teachers to make a holistic, best-fit judgement about a child's development, and their readiness for year 1. When forming a judgement about whether an individual child is at the expected level of development, teachers should draw on their knowledge of the child and their own expert professional judgement. This is sufficient evidence to assess a child's individual level of development in relation to each of the ELGs. Recorded written or photographic evidence is not required.

(DfE, 2024: 11–12)

1.
Personal, Social and Emotional development

As an Early Years teacher, it's essential to understand and support children in Personal, Social and Emotional development, a prime area of learning. Personal development for a child in Early Years is all about creating 'CHIRP' children. CHIRP is something I made up to describe to parents what we hope Early Years children are by the end of the school year*:

'Confident, Happy, Independent, Resilient and Proud'

*Remembering that all children learn at different rates and have their own strengths, it is our job to support them in discovering them during this vital year.

Social development focuses on how children interact with others and the social structure they form, from relationships with others, communication skills, cooperation and conflict resolution. I appreciate and agree with you that this is so hard to 'teach'. These situations and teaching moments usually come during provision and are very much in the moment. But providing the vocabulary children can use in the moment, and taking the time to talk through the issue that has occurred, will enable you to pass on these skills to the children.

Emotional development is quite simply the children understanding their own emotions and how their actions can affect others. However, although I say 'quite simply', this is not simple at all. This year, I have introduced the zones of regulation to support sharing children's emotions. This is where the four colours (blue, green, yellow and red) represent feelings. We have started basic, with the colours representing just one feeling (sad, happy, worried and angry) for now and these will develop throughout the year. Top tip: Using the characters from *Inside Out* with one of the colours and emotions has also supported the children to visually connect them. Once the children have expressed their emotion, it's the turn of teachers or parents; this is the teaching moment. Recognise the emotion (everyone has the right to feel the way we do) then make suggestions about what we can do or teach to support the child in regulating back into the green zone. It may be breathing, it may be ripping up cardboard, it may be a cuddle, it may be needing to be heard and listened to, etc.

Personal, Social and Emotional development is all about equipping children with essential life skills that will serve as a foundation for their future relationships and wellbeing. Remember, every child is unique and their development will look different. In this section of the book you will discover ideas and activities to support your little learners, from self regulation, to creating a positive self-image, independence, understanding their emotions, and so much more.

"

Children's personal, social and emotional development is crucial for children to lead healthy and happy lives, and is fundamental to their cognitive development. Underpinning their personal development are the important attachments that shape their social world. Strong, warm and supportive relationships with adults enable children to learn how to understand their own feelings and those of others. Children should be supported to manage emotions, develop a positive sense of self, set themselves simple goals, have confidence in their own abilities, to persist and wait for what they want and direct attention as necessary. Through adult modelling and guidance, they will learn how to look after their bodies, including healthy eating, and manage personal needs independently. Through supported interaction with other children, they learn how to make good friendships, co-operate and resolve conflicts peaceably. These attributes will provide a secure platform from which children can achieve at school and in later life.

(DfE, 2024: 9)

Learning objectives for Personal, Social and Emotional development

The following list of learning objectives is from *Development Matters* (DfE, 2023a):

- Identify and moderate their own feelings socially and emotionally

- Manage their own needs: personal hygiene

- Know and talk about the different factors that support their overall health and wellbeing: regular physical activity; healthy eating; toothbrushing; sensible amounts of 'screen time'; having a good sleep routine; being a safe pedestrian

- See themselves as a valuable individual

- Show resilience and perseverance in the face of challenge

- Build constructive and respectful relationships

- Express their feelings and consider the feelings of others

- Think about the perspectives of others.

Early Learning Goals for Personal, Social and Emotional development

ELG: Self-Regulation

The following list is developed from *Early Years Foundation Stage Profile: 2024 handbook* (DfE 2023b: Annex A: 24–28):

- Show an understanding of their own feelings and those of others, and begin to regulate their behaviour accordingly

- Set and work towards simple goals, being able to wait for what they want and control their immediate impulses when appropriate

- Give focused attention to what the teacher says, responding appropriately even when engaged in activity, and show an ability to follow instructions involving several ideas or actions.

ELG: Managing Self

- Be confident to try new activities and show independence, resilience and perseverance in the face of challenge

- Explain the reasons for rules, know right from wrong and try to behave accordingly

- Manage their own basic hygiene and personal needs, including dressing, going to the toilet and understanding the importance of healthy food choices.

ELG: Building Relationships

- Work and play cooperatively and take turns with others

- Form positive attachments to adults and friendships with peers

- Show sensitivity to their own and to others' needs.

Toothbrushing

Learning objective: Know and talk about the different factors that support their overall health and wellbeing: Toothbrushing
ELG: Managing Self

Resources you will need

Activity 1

- Printed laminated picture of teeth
- Whiteboard pen
- Toothbrush (and toothpaste, as an added extra).

Activity 2

- Empty 2l cola bottles
- White paint
- Hot glue gun
- Cardboard
- Playdough
- Toothbrush
- Floss.

Step-by-step instructions

Activity 1 – Cleaning teeth (using a laminated picture)

- Laminate your printed teeth picture (so it can be used over and over again; alternatively you can use a dry wipe wallet)
- Use the whiteboard pen to make marks on the teeth to create plaque
- Ask the children, 'Can you use the toothbrush to clean your teeth?' As an added extra, you could get the children to use toothpaste too.

Activity 2 – Cleaning teeth (using cola bottles)

- Cut the bottles so you just have the bottom of them
- Paint them white
- Use a hot glue gun to stick them down onto the cardboard in a mouth shape
- Place the playdough between all of the sections to represent plaque
- Get the children to use the toothbrush and floss to clean the teeth.

Key vocabulary and questions

- Teeth/tooth
- Floss
- Toothbrush/toothpaste
- Clean/brush.

Adaptations which can be made

- Ask the children, 'Can you clean all of the teeth in two minutes?' Use a sand timer to represent the amount of time you should clean your teeth for.

Top tips

- A visit from a local dentist is also a great opportunity for the children to learn about oral health. Get in contact with your local dental surgery and see if they are willing to make a visit.
- Colgate's website has many free resources to download (www.colgateprofessional.co.uk/resources/resources-for-patients/children-oral-care).

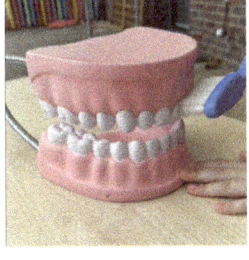

Figure 1.1 Using a giant toothbrush on a model mouth is a fun way to help children get to grips with this skill

Figure 1.2 Timing the children during the activity will help them to learn how long they should clean their teeth for

Figure 1.3 Using a whiteboard marker to create 'plaque' means you can use the printed teeth many times over

Figure 1.4 A fun activity using cola bottles, or anything you can get your hands on, will help children engage with learning this important skill

Sleep

Learning objective: Know and talk about the different factors that support their overall health and wellbeing: regular physical activity, healthy eating, toothbrushing, sensible amounts of 'screen time', having a good sleep routine, being a safe pedestrian
ELG: Managing Self

Resources you will need

Activity 1

- Paper plate
- Scissors
- Hole punch
- Wool
- Feathers.

Activity 2

- Bedtime sequencing cards with words or phrases on them such as 'toothbrushing', 'toilet', 'wash face', 'story time', 'put PJs on'.

Activity 3

- Stick or twig
- Wool
- Marker pen.

Step-by-step instructions

Activity 1 – Dreamcatcher

- Using the scissors, cut out the middle of the paper plate
- Use the hole punch to make holes around the outside section of the plate
- Now thread the wool in and out of the holes and across the centre
- Thread a hanging piece of wool at the bottom and tie on the feathers.

Activity 2 – Sequencing bedtime timetable

- Print off the steps you take before going to bed. Ask the children, 'Can you put these in order? What do you do first? Next? Last?'
- Listen to the feedback of the children and how children may do things differently.

Activity 3 – Worry doll

- Break the sticks into pieces about 5cm in length
- Use wool to wrap around and around the stick and then secure it
- Use the marker to make a face on the stick.

Discussions these activities might bring up to extend learning

- What time do we wake up?
- How much sleep do we need?
- Why do we need to sleep?
- What happens to our bodies while we sleep?
- What happens if we don't sleep?

Figure 1.5   Making a dreamcatcher from a paper plate, string and feathers is a creative activity and can also help prompt conversations about the importance of sleep

Figure 1.6   Picture cards help a child learn to order their bedtime routine

Figure 1.7   A large lollipop stick can be used to create a worry doll

Figure 1.8   A child holding their finished worry doll

Road safety

Learning objective: Know and talk about the different factors that support their overall health and wellbeing: regular physical activity, healthy eating, toothbrushing, sensible amounts of 'screen time', having a good sleep routine, being a safe pedestrian
ELG: Managing Self

Resources you will need

Activity 1

- Coloured paper (red, yellow, green and black)
- Scissors
- Glue.

Activity 2

- Chalk
- Bikes and scooters
- 'Lollypop person' yellow jacket.

Step-by-step instructions

Activity 1 – The traffic light game in PE

This is to teach the children what the traffic light colours mean for independent play in provision.

Make your own traffic lights by using the coloured paper to cut out circles to represent the traffic lights:

- Red = stop (stand still)
- Amber = get ready
- Green = go (run).

Call out the different colours and change movement accordingly

Ask the children, 'Can you remember what order they go in?'

Activity 2 – Road safety (Stop, look and listen)

- Use the chalk on the playground or outside area to mark out the road
- Use the bikes and scooters to play along the road. Ask the children, 'Where are the paths? Where do we need to go to cross safety?'
- You can also include a 'lollypop person' if this is representative of your local area.

This activity can also be replicated within the small work area of your classroom.

Key vocabulary and questions

- Stop, look, listen
- Road/path
- Safe/safety
- How can I stay safe on the road, or on the path?

Figure 1.9 Knowing what the different colours of a traffic light denote is an important road safety skill

Building independent skills

Learning objective: Know and talk about the different factors that support their overall health and wellbeing
ELG: Managing Self

Resources you will need

Activity 1

- Dressing-up costumes
- Jumpers.

Activity 3

- Children's coats.

Activity 5

- Visuals – steps for home time.

Activity 2

- Old clothing such as coats, jumpers, shoes, etc.

Activity 4

- Hair scrunchies.

Step-by-step instructions

Activity 1 – Getting dressed

- Dressing and undressing yourself is a big skill to learn and involves so many other elements and all it takes is practice and more practice
- To support children doing this, it's really about giving them step-by-step clear instructions to support them, as well as time
- This can be done within the classroom by dressing up in costumes
- Another way of supporting children during these early years of their life is teaching them how to put jumper sleeves in the right way.

Activity 2 – Fastenings

- Practise with different fastenings, such as velcro, zips, buttons, lace-ups and poppers. This could be done by bringing in old clothing such as shirts, coats and shoes.

Activity 3 – Coat flip/zip

Provide the children with the following step-by-step instructions:

- Place your coat on the floor with the hood by your feet
- Put your hands into the arm holes and hold on
- Lift the coat over the top of your head and push your arms through the holes
- Now have a practice of doing up your zip. Practise this step by step. First link in the two pieces, then hold with one hand and pull the zip up with the other hand. This is easier to practise on someone else.

Activity 4 – Socks

Provide the children with the following instructions to practise putting socks on. This is the same action as putting socks on so will support this learning:

- Take off your shoes and practise putting scrunchies onto your legs.

Activity 5 – Responsibility for belongings

- As children get into school, they have to be responsible for their own belongings. This means they may need a reminder about what they need to get before the end of the day. Using visuals will support their learning in this.

Figure 1.10 Practising with different types of fastenings is important

Figure 1.11 Buttoning up a shirt can be tricky to master

Figure 1.12 It is important to give children clear instructions to help them learn how to dress and undress

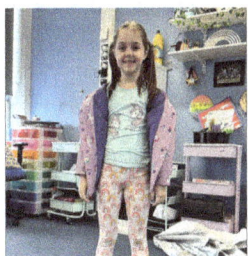

Figure 1.13 Children will grow in confidence if they are supported and given lots of time to practise dressing and undressing

Hand-washing experiment

Learning objective: Know and talk about the different factors that support their overall health and wellbeing
ELG: Managing Self

Resources you will need

- Tray
- Black pepper
- Liquid soap
- Water.

Step-by-step instructions

Provide the children with the following instructions:

- Pour the water onto the tray

- Sprinkle black pepper into the water (it will lay on top of the water)

- Dip your finger into the mixture.* Ask the children, 'Can you see how the pepper sticks to your fingers?' Point out that this is like germs and that if you then touch other things, the germs will spread

- Now squirt a little liquid soap onto your finger and dip it into the mixture. The pepper will be repelled by the soap and move.

*If you do not wish to dip your finger into this, then use a cotton bud.

Key vocabulary and questions

- Germs
- Spread
- Clean/wash
- Why is it important to wash our hands with soap?
- What happens if we don't use soap when washing our hands?
- How should we wash our hands?
- How should we move our hands when washing them?

Figure 1.14   Learning about germs made fun with the use of ground pepper

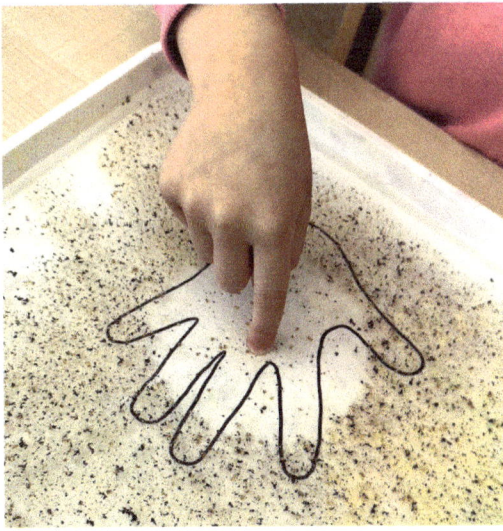

Figure 1.15   Using their finger (or a cotton bud) helps the child see how germs can stick to them, and then spread

Toilet wiping

Learning objective: Know and talk about the different factors that support their overall health and wellbeing
ELG: Managing Self

Resources you will need

- Two balloons
- Masking tape
- Chair
- Toilet roll/wipes
- Optional: chocolate spread.

Step-by-step instructions

- Attach the two balloons to the back of the chair using masking tape

- Get the child to sit on the chair and use the toilet roll or wipes to practise wiping between the balloons

- Optional: add a small amount of chocolate spread between the balloons. Ask the child, 'Did you wipe away all of the chocolate spread? Does it all go with one wipe?'

- This is a more secure way for children to practise wiping and the action of twisting their bodies around and wiping with one hand.

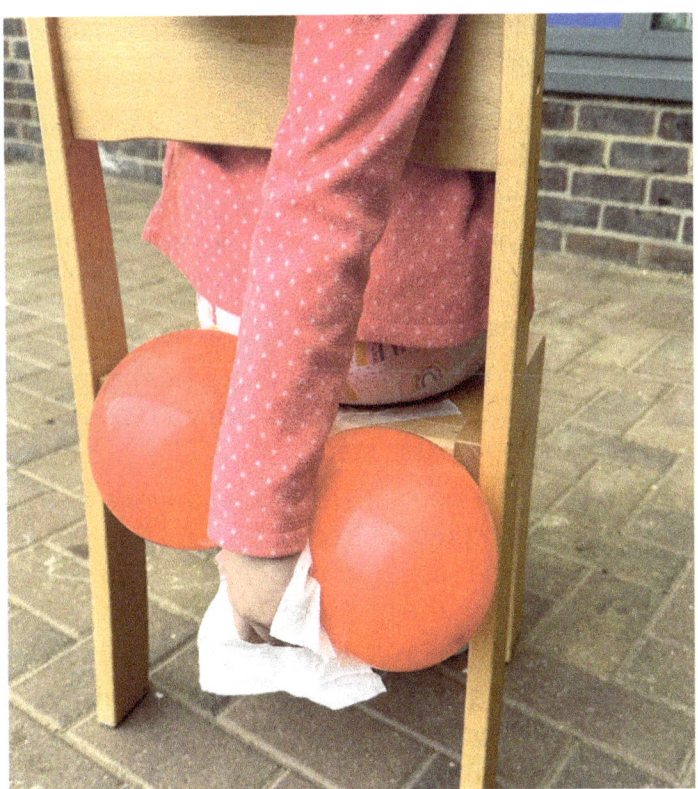

Figure 1.16   Using a wet wipe to wipe between balloons is a creative way for children to practise toilet wiping

Turn-taking role play

Learning objectives: Build constructive and respectful relationships; Identify and moderate their own feelings socially and emotionally

ELGs: Building Relationships; Self-Regulation

Resources you will need

- A toy/resource
- Teaching Assistant (TA).

Step-by-step instructions

This would be taught as an input to discuss why we should share and strategies to use if others don't share with us.

- Ask your TA to come up to the front of the class with you and explain that today we are going to talk about sharing and taking turns

- Ask your TA to play with a toy. Ask the children, 'If Mrs X is playing with this and I want to have a go, should I just go and take it from her?' (Take the toy away. This usually gets quite the shocked reaction out of the children!)

- Ask the children for strategies you could use instead of just taking the toy

- One suggestion would be to ask for it: you play with the toy and your TA asks, 'Can I have a go?' Shout back 'No!' and turn your back. A child may suggest saying 'please'. Repeat this step

- Ask the children, 'If they still won't share it, does anyone else have any other ideas?' Another suggestion could be to count down. Ask, 'What could I get to count down?' Children may suggest a timer. Ask them which colour of time they'd use (i.e., how long they think a turn should be). You can explain, 'Once the timer runs out, then it will be my go'

- Ask the children, 'If you have tried all of these things and they still aren't sharing, what should you do now?' You can explain that now would be the time to come and speak with a teacher.

Top tips

- Turn-taking can take place in every area of your classroom, inside and outside
- Good turn-taking resources include board games and puzzles
- Strategies to support turn taking include:
  - Asking – social phrases
  - Timers
  - Arrow – adding a visual arrow to whose go it is during a board game can support children who find it difficult to wait their turn.

Figure 1.17   Using timers of different durations is a great way to help children with the skill of turn-taking

Drawing yourself

Learning objective: See themselves as a valuable individual
ELGs: Building Relationships; Self-Regulation

Resources you will need

- Large backing paper
- Scissors
- Cup
- Felt pens
- Mirrors.

Step-by-step instructions

- Cut out the large backing paper to the size of the table or tray
- Draw circles around the paper using the cup as a guideline
- Invite the children to draw themselves. Ask them, 'What colours are you going to use?'
- The children can use the mirrors to support finding out about themselves, for example noticing the colour of their eyes
- Invite the children to show different emotions, saying for example, 'Can you make a happy face?'

Key vocabulary and questions

- Names of colours
- Shapes/movements of lines, e.g. up, down, around, curly, straight.

Adaptations which can be made

- Invite the children to write their name next to their picture. This could make a great display piece for your class
- Ask them to add on their body
- Suggest to the children that they draw an alien. Ask them, for example 'What shapes are you going to use? How many legs are you going to add?'

Figure 1.18   Use colouring pens to invite children to draw a face and an emotion

Breathing techniques

Learning objectives: Identify and moderate their own feelings socially and emotionally; Express their feelings and consider the feelings of others
ELG: Self-Regulation

Resources you will need

- Feather
- Picture of a star
- Picture of a rainbow
- Hoberman sphere
- Rotating disco ball light.

Step-by-step instructions

- Use the different pictures to provide guidance to the children on regulating their breathing. For example, you could instruct the children, 'Put your finger on the rainbow, and breathe in through your nose as you follow the rainbow up, and breathe out through your mouth as you follow it down with your finger'

- Get the children to use the feather to stroke down their arms. Ask them, 'How does it feel? Can you blow the feather off your hand? Ready, 1, 2, 3, blow. How far does it go?'

These are strategies to teach the children to help them relax. You can also help to explain when they might want to use them.

Key vocabulary and questions

- Calm/relaxed
- Breath in/out
- Deep breath
- Blow.

Other activities to try

- Lie down and watch the disco lights. Ask the children, 'What colours can you see?'
- Listen to relaxing music to ground yourself
- Turn on a lava lamp and watch the lava bubbles go up and down
- Listen to music and make movements along your body. For example, pitter-patter raindrops along your legs, spiders crawling up your arms, or circles on your tummy
- Story massage (make sure you ask permission from the person you are doing it to).

Figure 1.19   A visual aid can help children to be mindful of their breathing

Figure 1.20   This marble placed on a wave is pushed along while the child is breathing

Figure 1.21   An expandable breathing sphere is pulled out when breathing in through the nose ...

Figure 1.22   ... And pushed in when breathing out through their mouth

Giving it a go

Learning objective: Show resilience and perseverance in the face of challenge
ELG: Self-Regulation

Resources you will need

Activity 1

- Tuff tray
- Water
- Plank of wood (spare decking was once donated which has been great for this!).

Activity 2

- Mobilio pieces
- Masking tape
- Pipe cleaners
- Scissors.

Step-by-step instructions

Activity 1 – Walk the plank

- Pour the water into the tray and place the wooden plank on top of the tray
- Ask a child, 'Can you walk along the plank and not fall off into the water?'
- The children love this one and cheer, 'Walk the plank!'

This is a great activity to go with a pirate theme, when you could also make treasure maps.

Activity 2 – Construction without connectors

- Place the Mobilio onto the tray but take away all of the connecting pieces
- This is so the children can problem-solve. Ask them, 'How are you going to connect them? What can you use?' This can be open-ended, or you could give some options to try, such as masking tape and pipe cleaners
- Ask the children, 'Which makes the best connector? Or can *you* find something to connect the pieces together?'

Key vocabulary and questions

- Try again
- It's okay to make mistakes
- Never mind, I can try again.

Figure 1.23 Encouraging a child to 'walk the plank' can challenge them to give something a go that might be nerve-wracking

Figure 1.24 A car built from mobilio using pipe cleaners instead of connectors

Circle games

Learning objectives: See themselves as a valuable individual; Build constructive and respectful relationships
ELG: Building Relationships

Resources you will need

Activity 1

- Ball
- Soft toy.

Step-by-step instructions

These games are great to play at the beginning of the year to encourage the learning of names and building a sense of belonging.

Activity 1 – Pass the _____?

- Ask a child, 'Can you roll the ball to _____ (enter name)?' or 'Can you pass the soft toy to _____ (enter name)?'
- This can include any object, so you can also add in some extra sneaky learning, for example using number flashcards: 'Can you pass the number 3 to _____ (enter name)?'
- This concept can also be used with non-physical things, for example: 'Can you pass the smile around the circle?'
- The person who starts smiles to the person on the right of them. They smile back and pass it on to the next person on the right until the smile gets passed all around the circle
- It's best to start with a physical object to pass before moving to the more abstract, which could include smiles, claps or high fives.

As you get more adventurous, and if you have space, you can introduce circle games, such as duck duck goose or fruit salad.

Activity 2 – Catchphrase

- Take a photo of the children in your class (one by one)
- Upload these to a PowerPoint presentation and add different shapes over the top
- One by one, remove the shapes. Ask the class if they can guess who is hiding underneath. Ask them, 'How did you know who was hiding?'
- This game can be played with so many variations, such as areas of the classroom, numbers, letters, animals, etc.

Activity 3 – Who's talking?

- Everyone closes their eyes (make sure there's no cheating!)
- Tap the shoulder of one child who should open their eyes and say the phrase, 'apple pie and custard' (Honestly no idea why we say this, I just always have, but you can use any phrase!)
- Everyone then opens their eyes and has to guess who said the phrase
- The more you play this game, the better the children get at disguising their voices.

I am special because ...

Step-by-step instructions

Activities are usually completed during a circle time where we discuss similarities and differences between us. For example, 'What colour hair do you have? Do you have a pet? Is your favourite colour pink?' Try the following:

- Get the children active while asking them questions, for example, 'Do you have a brother? If so, stand here. If you don't have a brother, stand here'. (I have also seen this done successfully with a parachute, where children run across to the other side if the answer to the question is that they do have a brother, for example)

- Ask the children to complete the sentence, 'I am special because ...' Let them loose and see what they come up with – I love hearing their responses!

- Every week in my class we have a 'special person'. This means they have achieved something during the week which we are really proud of. We share this within the class and say, 'You are special because ...' followed by the reason. Then it is opened up to the rest of the class to say reasons why they believe this person is special and it's just beautiful to listen to them. Don't get me wrong, this takes A LOT of practising at the beginning of the year to not hear, 'You are special because I like your shoes' or ' You are special because I like playing with you'. But by mid year they have usually got great at coming up with reasons for why that person is special

- In addition to the above activity, to make it extra special we have used things such as the 'special person cape' to wear whenever they like during the week. Or, they are allowed to sit on a special cushion/chair during carpet time

- It's just the most precious thing to observe the children being proud and talking positively about each other.

2.
Communication and language

Communication and language development does exactly what it says, it's all about the communication and language a child learns through listening, attention, speaking and understanding. It is essential for teachers and parents to understand and support children in these skills, as a prime area of learning.

Communication and language clearly go hand in hand in a child's development. As well as communicating through language and gestures, children can also communicate through mark-making. Through positive relationships, children can respond to verbal and nonverbal interactions as they anticipate and initiate communication with others. Children observe so much and will then use what they have seen to use within their own play, such as role playing as 'parents' or going to the shops.

Singing nursery rhymes is such a critical part of building language and will help children segment words into syllables, hear similarities between words that rhyme and initial sounds. Nursery rhymes are important for language acquisition and support speech development. Listening comprehension is a foundational skill that is often not given enough importance within schools, so sing, sing, sing, and repeat and repeat!

Listening and attention is part of this area of development too. Around this age children should be able to concentrate for double their age. For example, a reception-aged child would be focused for a maximum time of 8–10 minutes. No matter what you say, mine is definitely not double my age now, so I don't know when this stops!

The development of children's spoken language underpins all seven areas of learning and development. Children's back-and-forth interactions from an early age form the foundations for language and cognitive development. The number and quality of the conversations they have with adults and peers throughout the day in a language-rich environment is crucial. By commenting on what children are interested in or doing, and echoing back what they say with new vocabulary added, practitioners will build children's language effectively. Reading frequently to children, and engaging them actively in stories, non-fiction, rhymes and poems, and then providing them with extensive opportunities to use and embed new words in a range of contexts, will give children the opportunity to thrive. Through conversation, story-telling and role play, where children share their ideas with support and modelling from their teacher, and sensitive questioning that invites them to elaborate, children become comfortable using a rich range of vocabulary and language structures.

(DfE, 2024: 9)

A daily story time is essential in any Early Years classroom. This could be fiction or non-fiction, but also don't forget the use of puppets, non-worded books and making up stories on the spot.

However, when a child decides to communicate with you (verbally, non-verbally, gestures, though their behaviour) ensure you are acknowledging that communication and supporting them as necessary.

Learning objectives for communication and language

The following extract is taken from *Development Matters* (DfE, 2023a: 56–58):

- Understand how to listen carefully and why listening is important

- Learn new vocabulary

- Use new vocabulary throughout the day

- Ask questions to find out more and to check they understand what has been said to them

- Use new vocabulary in different contexts

- Listen carefully to rhymes and songs, paying attention to how they sound

- Learn rhymes, poems and songs

- Engage in non-fiction books

- Articulate their ideas and thoughts in well-formed sentences

- Connect one idea or action to another using a range of connectives

- Describe events in some detail

- Use talk to help work out problems and organise thinking and activities to explain how things work and why they might happen

- Develop social phrases

- Engage in story times

- Listen to and talk about stories to build familiarity and understanding

- Retell the story, once they have developed a deep familiarity with the text, some as exact repetition and some in their own words

- Listen to and talk about selected non-fiction to develop a deep familiarity with new knowledge and vocabulary.

Early Learning Goals for communication and language

ELG: Listening, Attention and Understanding

The following list is developed from *Early Years Foundation Stage Profile: 2024 handbook* (DfE 2023b: Annex A: 24):

- Listen attentively and respond to what they hear with relevant questions, comments and actions when being read to and during whole class discussions and small group interactions

- Make comments about what they have heard and ask questions to clarify their understanding

- Hold conversation when engaged in back-and-forth exchanges with their teacher and peers.

ELG: Speaking

- Participate in small group, class and one-to-one discussions, offering their own ideas, using recently introduced vocabulary

- Offer explanations for why things might happen, making use of recently introduced vocabulary from stories, non-fiction, rhymes and poems when appropriate

- Express their ideas and feelings about their experiences using full sentences, including use of past, present and future tenses and making use of conjunctions, with modelling and support from their teacher.

Book corner

Learning objectives: Understand how to listen carefully and why listening is important; Learn new vocabulary; Use new vocabulary throughout the day; Engage in non-fiction books; Engage in story times; Listen to and talk about stories to build familiarity and understanding; Retell the story, once they have developed a deep familiarity with the text, some as exact repetition and some in their own words; Listen to and talk about selected non-fiction to develop a deep familiarity with new knowledge and vocabulary

ELGs: Listening, Attention and Understanding; Speaking

Resources you will need

- Story books
- Non-fiction books
- Comics
- Magazines.

Step-by-step instructions

- It's really not about 'teaching' with these activities, but rather about children being exposed to different types of texts and how to use them. For example, non-fiction books are where we can find information, we can find what we want to from looking at a contents page and we can move around the book (not page by page)

- Magazines: Ask parents for donations of these and either laminate the pages or pop them inside dry wipe wallets so they can be reused over and over (because these are always popular, including the puzzle pages)

- Story books (fiction): Not only is there a huge art in storytelling with books, but when reading a story you also discuss any new vocabulary which may appear, as well as settings, characters, and the beginning/middle/end of the story.

Reading corners

I would suggest having a range of books within a reading corner for the children to access and explore. It is also great to have books which link to the topic you are focusing on, as well as the classic stories children can retell over and over. However, I would also say it is important to explore books within other areas of the classroom too. For example, books around construction, building, or STEAM within the construction area.

Top tip

Create QR codes within your book area for children to access listening and watching stories independently using tablets.

Figure 2.1 Having a space such as a reading corner encourages children to explore a range of different books

Musical instruments

Learning objectives: Listen carefully to rhymes and songs, paying attention to how they sound; Learn rhymes, poems and songs
ELG: Listening, Attention and Understanding

Resources you will need

- Musical instruments such as bells, drums, xylophones, rainmakers
- Blanket.

Step-by-step instructions

- Introduce the instruments to the children and name them
- Get the children to listen carefully to which instrument is playing
- Place the instruments underneath the blanket and play one of them
- Ask the children, 'Which instrument was it?'
- Repeat using different instruments.

The children can easily replay this game independently within provision.

If your children are struggling with listening games, ensure these are only short games (a maximum of double their age in minutes) and in small groups or 1:1.

Figure 2.2   A child covering up a range of musical instruments with a blanket

Making musical shakers

Learning objectives: Listen carefully to rhymes and songs, paying attention to how they sound; Learn rhymes, poems and songs
ELG: Listening, Attention and Understanding

We don't need fancy musical instruments here in the Early Years. We are all about a good bit of DIY and getting the children involved!

Resources you will need

- Rice and/or lentils
- Empty jars or pots (jam jars are perfect!)
- Masking tape.

Step-by-step instructions

This is a great activity to complete in a small group.

- Depending on the jar/pot each child has, the first step is to decorate it. If you have a glass jar, using tissue paper and PVA glue makes a great texture and effect
- Add in rice to the inside and seal with a lid. In this example, I am using another paper cup for a lid and taping the two cups together to seal them
- Shake away!

Figure 2.3　A musical shaker can be made with a few simple ingredients

Figure 2.4　And it can be a lot of fun!

Listening walk

Learning objectives: Listen carefully to rhymes and songs, paying attention to how they sound; Learn rhymes, poems and songs
ELG: Listening, Attention and Understanding

Resources you will need

- An outside area
- Optional: a tick sheet with images of things you may hear outside.

Step-by-step instructions

- Take the children for a walk within your outside area
- Say, 'Let's listen carefully. What can you hear?'
- Start them off by describing what you can hear, for example, 'I can hear a bird. Let's tick it off on our sheets'
- Invite the children to notice what they can hear
- Extend this further by going for a walk in your local area. Ask, 'Are the sounds different? What else can you hear?'

Figure 2.5 Using images of different sounds children might hear on a listening walk can be a useful prompt

Describe and find the animal

Learning objectives: Listen carefully to rhymes and songs, paying attention to how they sound; Learn rhymes, poems and songs
ELG: Listening, Attention and Understanding

Resources you will need

- Models of animals.

Step-by-step instructions

- Lay out the animal models on the table
- Describe the animal until the children can guess which animal it is
- For example, 'This animal has four legs, this animal is black and white, this animal lives on the farm. Do you know which animal this is?'

The children can easily replay this game independently within provision.

To make this activity harder, get the children to ask questions about your animal but you can only answer yes or no, for example, 'Does your animal live under the sea?'

Figure 2.6 Describing different animals gives children the chance to practise their skills of listening, attention and understanding

Silly soup

Learning objectives: Listen carefully to rhymes and songs, paying attention to how they sound; Learn rhymes, poems and songs
ELG: Listening, Attention and Understanding

Resources you will need

- Objects which rhyme
- Bowl and spoon.

Step-by-step instructions

- This activity can be played with physical objects or abstractly without
- The rhyme to say is: 'I'm making lots of silly soup. I'm making soup that's silly. I'm going to cook it in the fridge. To make it nice and chilly. It goes ...' (then add your items of either rhyming or alliterative words).

Examples of rhyming words:

fox – box – socks

hat – cat – bat – rat – mat

wig – pig – dig

egg – peg – leg

hair – bear – chair

bed – red – head

frog – dog – log

spoon – moon – balloon

Examples of alliteration:

sausages – socks – soap – snake – spoon

beans – bananas – buttons – box – bottle – bag

fish – fork – fox – frying pan – five – frog

mirror – mug – money – mop – marmalade

doll – dinosaur – drum – dog – dice

Figure 2.7   A wide variety of items can go into the 'silly soup'

Clapping syllables

Learning objectives: Listen carefully to rhymes and songs, paying attention to how they sound; Learn rhymes, poems and songs
ELG: Listening, Attention and Understanding

Resources you will need

- Optional: claves, drum
- I would suggest noting down some words before completing this activity so you don't get stuck on the spot.

Step-by-step instructions

- Ask a child to clap out the correct number of syllables for a particular word (I always start with the child's name)
- For every syllable, the child makes a clap or bangs the drum
- A great song to link to, 'Clap it Out', can be found on GoNoodle
- If the child is finding it difficult to clap out a word, you could model it to them first to copy, or use their name, which is recognisable to them.

Figure 2.8   Learning about syllables is made easier for children through use of rhythm

Sing it back

Learning objectives: Listen carefully to rhymes and songs, paying attention to how they sound; Learn rhymes, poems and songs
ELG: Listening, Attention and Understanding

Step-by-step instructions

- Lead the children in warming up their voices. Say, 'Let's warm up our voices to check we are ready: blowing, sucking, tongue-stretching and wiggling. Copy my voice':

    o   Make your voice go down the slide – 'weeeeee'

    o   Make your voice bounce like a ball – 'boing, boing'

    o   Make your voice ring the bell – 'ding dong'

    o   Hiss like a snake – 'sssssss'

    o   Moo like a cow – 'moooooo'

    o   Be a steam train – 'choo choo'

    o   Be a clock – 'tick tock'

    o   Buzz like a bee – 'zzzzzz'

    o   Keep everyone quiet – 'shhhhh'

Figure 2.9   Singing is always a popular activity with children

Can you draw what I can draw?

Learning objectives: Ask questions to find out more and to check they understand what has been said to them; Articulate their ideas and thoughts in well-formed sentences; Connect one idea or action to another using a range of connectives; Use talk to help work out problems and organise thinking and activities to explain how things work and why they might happen
ELG: Listening, Attention and Understanding

Resources you will need

- Clipboard
- Paper
- Pencil.

Step-by-step instructions

The key to this activity is the language used and the instructions given.

- Each child should have a piece of paper and pencil (leaning on a clipboard will make this easier)
- Say, 'Listen carefully … I am going to tell you the shapes and lines you are going to draw but I'm not going to show you, and then we will see if it is the same at the end (it doesn't matter if it's not)'
- Now it's time to give the instructions. My top tip would be to start simple, e.g. a house, or a face, then move on to more abstract objects. Ensure your instructions are super clear. Consider the placement on the page, the size, the shape, etc.
- For example:
  o Draw a big square in the middle of your page
  o Inside the square at the bottom middle draw a rectangle with the long sides going up and the short sides across
  o Draw four squares within the large square

- Draw a large triangle on top of the large square
- What did yours look like?

If you want to make this activity easier:

- Start by creating a grid on a page. This can be as simple as four squares, or more complex if you like. The key here is going to be a focus on learning the vocabulary, such as the positional language of the page (top, bottom, side, corner, etc.)
- Ask the children, 'Can you draw a circle in the corner? Can you draw a blue triangle at the bottom?', and so on.

Adaptations which can be made

Can the children use their vocabulary to describe an image to each other to draw? This could be something they could think of independently, or you could have simple outline picture cards for them to use.

Figure 2.10   Creating a grid for children to draw in will help them in learning simple positional language

Sequencing

Learning objectives: Listen to and talk about stories to build familiarity and understanding; Retell the story, once they have developed a deep familiarity with the text, some as exact repetition and some in their own words

ELGs: Listening, Attention and Understanding; Speaking

Resources you will need

Sequencing picture cards, (minimum of two images) such as:

- Eating an apple
- Going down a slide
- Drinking a glass of water
- Eating a banana
- Making a bed
- Having a bath
- A tree growing
- Drawing a picture
- Building a snowman
- Making a sandwich
- Blowing a bubble.

Step-by-step instructions

- Place the set of sequencing cards onto the table
- Draw onto a picture of paper: 'First, Next, Last'
- Ask the children, 'What happens first?' Place this into the box labelled 'First'
- Repeat throughout the activity.

Key vocabulary and questions

- First
- Next
- Last.

Adaptations which can be made

This activity can link into retelling a story. 'What happened first, or at the beginning? What happened next? What happened at the end?' This could be via Small World play to retell the story of sequencing and retelling through images.

If your child is struggling with this activity, bring it back to basics where you have just two pictures, first and last. This can then be built up over time.

Figure 2.11   Sequencing language being taught through use of images

3.
Physical
development

Physical development is split into two sub sections of motor skills; fine and gross. These are simply the small and large movements of our body.

Gross motor skills are the large muscle movements and fine motor skills are the small muscle movements. It is important to note that motor skills are learnt abilities, so this means we aren't born with them, that is why they are critical to children's early development. So how do we teach them? Through practise, repetition and most importantly PLAY! Gross motor skills are used in PE for running, climbing, throwing and catching as well as so much more whereas fine motor skills are precision-based such as: threading, using pipettes, hama beads and using pegs. Most importantly, it's so vital to get practising these motor skills to then finally support letter formation and writing. Fine motor activities are one of my favourites to do with the children as you can encompass so many other learning opportunities within the activity too. The importance of fine motor skills can never be underestimated in linking to the skills of writing.

Physical activity is vital in children's all-round development, enabling them to pursue happy, healthy and active lives. Gross and fine motor experiences develop incrementally throughout early childhood, starting with sensory explorations and the development of a child's strength, coordination and positional awareness through tummy time, crawling and play movement with both objects and adults. By creating games and providing opportunities for play both indoors and outdoors, adults can support children to develop their core strength, stability, balance, spatial awareness, coordination and agility. Gross motor skills provide the foundation for developing healthy bodies and social and emotional well-being. Fine motor control and precision helps with hand–eye coordination, which is later linked to early literacy. Repeated and varied opportunities to explore and play with small world activities, puzzles, arts and crafts and the practice of using small tools, with feedback and support from adults, allow children to develop proficiency, control and confidence.

(DfE, 2024: 10)

Learning objectives for physical development

The following list of learning objectives is from *Development Matters* (DfE, 2023a: 68–73):

- Revise and refine the fundamental movement skills they have already acquired: rolling, crawling, walking, jumping, running, hopping, skipping, climbing

- Progress towards a more fluent style of moving, with developing control and grace

- Develop the overall body strength, coordination, balance and agility needed to engage successfully with future physical education sessions and other physical disciplines including dance, gymnastics, sport and swimming

- Use their core muscle strength to achieve a good posture when sitting at a table or sitting on the floor

- Combine different movements with ease and fluency

- Confidently and safely use a range of large and small apparatus indoors and outside, alone and in a group

- Develop overall body-strength, balance, coordination and agility

- Further develop and refine a range of ball skills including: throwing, catching, kicking, passing, batting, and aiming

- Develop confidence, competence, precision and accuracy when engaging in activities that involve a ball

- Develop their small motor skills so that they can use a range of tools competently, safely and confidently. Suggested tools: pencils for drawing and writing, paint brushes, scissors, knives, forks and spoons

- Develop the foundations of a handwriting style which is fast, accurate and efficient

- Further develop the skills they need to manage the school day successfully: lining up and queuing; mealtimes.

Early Learning Goals for physical development

ELG: Gross Motor Skills

The following list is developed from *Early Years Foundation Stage Profile: 2024 handbook* (DfE 2023b: Annex A: 25):

- Negotiate space and obstacles safely, with consideration for themselves and others

- Demonstrate strength, balance and coordination when playing

- Move energetically, such as running, jumping, dancing, hopping, skipping and climbing.

ELG: Fine Motor Skills

- Hold a pencil effectively in preparation for fluent writing – using the tripod grip in almost all cases

- Use a range of small tools, including scissors, paint brushes and cutlery

- Begin to show accuracy and care when drawing.

Spider web

Learning objective: Revise and refine the fundamental movement skills they have already acquired: rolling, crawling, walking, jumping, running, hopping, skipping, climbing
ELG: Gross Motor Skills

Resources you will need

- Barrier tape
- Obstacles.

Step-by-step instructions

- Use the barrier tape to tie around different obstacles
- Carefully navigate your way around the spider web. The children can climb over and under the obstacles as they work to get from one side to the other
- Ask the children, 'Can you move around the tape without getting caught? How do you move? Over? Under? Through?'

This activity can be recreated inside or outside.

Key vocabulary and questions

- Positional language, e.g. over, under, through
- Which way are you going to go?

Adaptations which can be made

Change the amount of tape you use to create larger or smaller spaces to move through.

Figure 3.1 Barrier tape can be used to make a 'spider's web', either inside or outside

Ball skills

Learning objectives: Further develop and refine a range of ball skills including: throwing, catching, kicking, passing, batting, and aiming; Develop confidence, competence, precision and accuracy when engaging in activities that involve a ball
ELG: Gross Motor Skills

Children thrive in activities that offer just the right level of challenge – neither too easy nor too difficult.

Top tips when teaching ball skills

- Begin with activities where either the child or the ball remains stationary, such as throwing, catching, or kicking a stationary ball. Then progress to activities where both the child and the ball are in motion, like dribbling a football
- Utilise alternative items for throwing and catching, such as bubbles, balloons, or scarves, which descend more slowly and are easier to catch
- Opt for soft, air-filled balls with some flexibility, like beach balls, to reduce the risk of injury
- Start with larger balls and heavier bean bags, gradually transitioning to lighter, smaller balls as skills improve
- When using targets, start with larger targets and gradually decrease their size
- Begin with shorter distances between the child and the target or each other, then gradually increase the distances
- Initiate with slow ball movements, progressively increasing the speed over time.

Throwing to target

- Roll balls into a goal, starting with a large target and progressing to a smaller one, assessing how many points the child can score in a minute
- Skittles: Roll the ball to knock down skittles, starting with a large ball close to the skittles and gradually increasing the rolling distance
- Sock ball: Make balls from rolled-up socks or use bean bags, aiming to throw them into a hoop or various-sized boxes from increasing distances.

Other activities to try

- Balloon volleyball: Bat a balloon back and forth, aiming to pass it over/ under a washing line or using a racket for added challenge.

Catching

- Throw and catch: Toss a bean bag up to eye level and catch it with both hands, gradually increasing the height of the throw
- Bounce and catch: Bounce a large ball and catch it with two hands, progressing to smaller balls
- Kneeling catch: Kneel in front of the child and throw a ball for them to catch while kneeling.

Football skills

- Kicking: Practice kicking with each leg, aiming at widening goals that narrow as skills improve
- Penalty kick: Kick a football into a goal from a designated spot, gradually reducing the goal size
- Happy feet: Squeeze a ball between the feet and move them alternately forward like a penguin carrying an egg
- Dribbling: Tap the ball gently from one foot to the other, maintaining control and avoiding excessive speed
- Obstacle dribbling: Dribble the ball around obstacles while maintaining control and technique.

Figure 3.2   Targets can be made smaller as children develop their ball skills

Figure 3.3   Using different heights of hoops can vary the challenge

Playdough and cutlery

Learning objective: Develop their small motor skills so that they can use a range of tools competently, safely and confidently. Suggested tools: pencils for drawing and writing, paint brushes, scissors, knives, forks and spoons
ELG: Fine Motor Skills

Resources you will need

- Playdough
- Cutlery.

Step-by-step instructions

- Manipulate the playdough into food shapes, such as small balls to look like peas to scoop onto the fork, a sausage to cut up, etc
- Let the children explore the playdough and cutlery
- Model yourself using the cutlery and cutting the playdough.

Key vocabulary and questions

- Names of cutlery, e.g. knife, fork
- Cut, chop, slice, push, pull, squeeze, roll.

Adaptations which can be made

Playdough is also a great material to use for practising using scissors.

Figure 3.4   Using a knife and fork to practise cutting the playdough 'sausage'

Scissor skills with tissue paper

Learning objective: Develop their small motor skills so that they can use a range of tools competently, safely and confidently. Suggested tools: pencils for drawing and writing, paint brushes, scissors, knives, forks and spoons
ELG: Fine Motor Skills

Resources you will need

- Crepe paper/tissue paper/sugar paper
- Scissors
- Tape
- Table/tuff tray.

Step-by-step instructions

- Cut the crepe paper or tissue paper into strips and stick it to the table/tuff tray
- Ask the children, 'Can you cut snips of the crepe paper/tissue paper?' or 'Can you follow the pattern on the sugar paper?'

Key vocabulary and questions

- Cut, snip, straight, curved, wavy, zig-zag, around
- Right-handed/left-handed/spring scissors.

Figure 3.5   Cutting light material such as crepe paper is a great way to introduce children to scissor skills

How to draw

Learning objectives: Develop their small motor skills so that they can use a range of tools competently, safely and confidently. Suggested tools: pencils for drawing and writing, paintbrushes, scissors, knives, forks and spoons; Develop the foundations of a handwriting style which is fast, accurate and efficient
ELG: Fine Motor Skills

Resources you will need

- Paper
- Pencils
- Clipboard or something the children can lean on
- Whiteboard or interactive whiteboard to model drawing on.

Step-by-step instructions

- Model to the children a simple drawing, step-by-step, so the children can follow along. For example:

  - Draw a square in the middle of your paper
  - Then draw a triangle on top
  - Draw a small rectangular door in the bottom middle of your square then draw four square windows
  - Does your house look like mine?

- Consider different animals, people, or objects you can draw depending on the children's interests or topic, for example, a crown if your topic is 'kings and queens', or a dog if the children like Paw Patrol.

Key vocabulary and questions

- Listen/listening
- Instructions

- Sequencing language, e.g. first, then, next
- Curved, straight, big, small.

Adaptations which can be made

- Consider the difficulty of the picture you are going to draw, and try different difficulty levels
- Use colours for a purpose, adding colour to your picture or using different coloured pencils to draw different parts of the picture.

Figure 3.6   Once children have mastered their step-by-step drawings, why not add in colour?

Name-writing rocket

Learning objective: Develop the foundations of a hand writing style which is fast, accurate and efficient
ELG: Fine Motor Skills

Resources you will need

- Felt pens
- Glue
- Coloured paper
- Scissors.

Step-by-step instructions

Provide the children with the following instructions to make a rocket which spells out their name:

- On the paper, draw the top of the rocket (triangle)
- Cut the coloured paper into squares and write different letters on each square
- Find the letters which are in your name and stick them in order.

Key vocabulary and questions

- Sounds of letters
- First, next, last.

Adaptations which can be made

- This activity can easily be adapted into making word rockets with CVC, CCVC, and CVCC words on them
- Ask the children if they can make a rhyming rocket. Stick the rhyming words together.

Figure 3.7   Any word can be used in the writing rocket activity, but the child's name is a great place to start

Gross motor writing

Learning objectives: Confidently and safely use a range of large and small apparatus indoors and outside, alone and in a group; Develop overall body-strength, balance, coordination and agility; Develop the foundations of a handwriting style which is fast, accurate and efficient
ELG: Gross Motor Skills

Resources you will need

- Hockey sticks
- Paint
- Paint tray
- Large paint brushes
- Backing paper/sugar paper
- Masking tape.

Step-by-step instructions

Provide the children with the following instructions:

- Use the masking tape to attach the large paint brushes to the end of the hockey sticks
- Lay out the backing paper or sugar paper and dip the paint brush into the paint before then mark-making onto the paper.

This activity enables children to use their gross motor skills to control their movements.

Key vocabulary and questions

- Names of colours, e.g. red, blue, yellow, green
- Brush stroke
- What are you going to paint?
- Can you tell me about your painting?
- Can you make any of the patterns we've been practising?

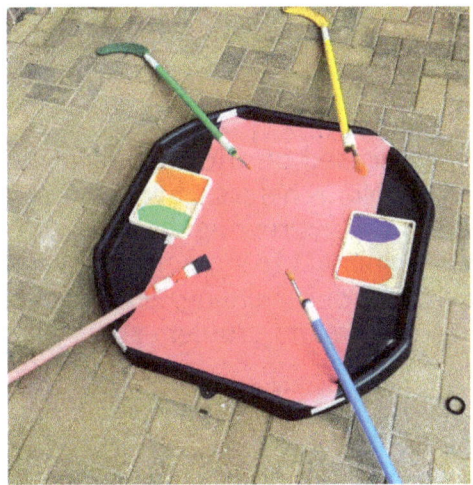

Figure 3.8   Using hockey sticks to help children develop their gross motor skills

Den building

Learning objectives: Confidently and safely use a range of large and small apparatus indoors and outside, alone and in a group; Develop overall body-strength, balance, coordination and agility; Develop their small motor skills so that they can use a range of tools competently, safely and confidently. Suggested tools: pencils for drawing and writing, paint brushes, scissors, knives, forks and spoons
ELGs: Gross Motor Skills, Fine Motor Skills

Creating dens is primarily focused on the journey of construction rather than solely on the final outcome. Nonetheless, children often showcase remarkable creativity and collaboration in constructing their dens!

As educators, our responsibility is to support this play by offering appropriate materials, designated areas for den-building, when to offer assistance and when to encourage children to explore and problem-solve independently.

Resources you will need

The space for play doesn't have to be extensive like a forest (although I must admit, I'm already envious if you have one!). A small garden area is perfectly adequate; what truly counts is not the size of the space but the learning and play opportunities it provides. Other useful resources for den-making include:

- Pegs
- Crates
- Material and tarpaulins
- Outdoor cushions
- Classroom chairs.

Step-by-step instructions

Now that you have your equipment ready, it's time to begin. However, it's important not to simply stand by and expect children to intuitively know how to utilise the equipment. Just like any hands-on learning experience, children benefit from exploring the resources, while adults should demonstrate how to use them effectively. As facilitators of learning, adults play a crucial role in modelling, extending play, inspiring creativity, and supporting ideas. Once children have observed and practised sharing ideas and using the equipment, they often demonstrate the ability to generate their own ideas, problem-solve, and engage in critical thinking – a testament to effective teaching and learning.

Benefits of den making include:

- Fostering imagination and role-playing scenarios
- Enhancing language skills through conversation, listening, and discussing den-building strategies
- Cultivating cooperation and negotiation skills by collaborating with others on constructing a den
- Developing physical abilities such as building, spatial awareness, and resource selection
- Practising calculation and estimation, gaining insights into size, space, shape, and measurement.

Figure 3.9   Den-building has huge benefits, including the opportunity to be outside

Threading

Learning objective: Develop their small motor skills so that they can use a range of tools competently, safely and confidently. Suggested tools: pencils for drawing and writing, paint brushes, scissors, knives, forks and spoons
ELG: Fine Motor Skills

Resources you will need

Activity 1

- Coloured, letter or number beads/Cheerios/pasta
- Pipe cleaners.

Activity 2

- Spaghetti (uncooked)/skewers
- Playdough
- Beads.

Step-by-step instructions

Activity 1

- Instruct the children to thread the bead onto the pipe cleaners
- Ask them, 'Can you put the numbers in order? Can you make your name, or a word, or even a tricky word? Can you make a repeating pattern?'

Activity 2

Instruct the children to:

- Roll a small ball of playdough and stick it to the table
- Add in a piece of spaghetti or a skewer into the playdough, standing up
- Place the beads onto the skewer. Ask the children, 'Can you make a repeating pattern?'

Key vocabulary and questions

- In, out, over, through, pull.

Adaptations which can be made

Make your own threading sheet by using a single hole punch with a laminated picture.

Figure 3.10   Threading is an important way of developing fine motor skills

Tweezers

Learning objective: Develop their small motor skills so that they can use a range of tools competently, safely and confidently. Suggested tools: pencils for drawing and writing, paint brushes, scissors, knives, forks and spoons
ELG: Fine Motor Skills

Resources you will need

- Tweezers
- Sorting objects
- Coloured bowls
- Activity 1 – colour sorting mat
- Activity 2 – masking tape.

Step-by-step instructions

Activity 1

- Put the coloured sorting mat with coloured bowls onto the tuff tray
- Spread out the sorting objects around the tray along with the tweezers
- Instruct the children to sort the objects into the correct coloured bowls using the tweezers.

Activity 2

- Spread out the sorting objects around the tuff tray
- Add masking tape over the top to create a spider's web
- Use the tweezers to get the sorting objects into the correct coloured bowls.

Adaptations which can be made

Using a sand timer, challenge the children to complete as many as they can in two minutes. Or ask them, for example, 'Can you get all of the green ones?'

Figure 3.11   Selecting various different objects for the children to sort using tweezers is another great way to help develop fine motor skills

4.
Literacy

Literacy development is split into three sub sections: comprehension, reading and writing. Here, we are looking at what the children understand about spoken English language, whether children can read according to the phonics scheme taught in school, and whether they write phonetically plausible sentences.

The progress children make during their reception year in writing, from pre-writing patterns to full sentences, is mind-blowing! The development of phonics, learning single sounds, blending, letter formation, writing CVC words to full sentences ... it's a magical progress, and in observing these developments, it's always the proudest I feel.

However, it's also the hardest (in my opinion) to plan enhancements and get the children excited for. The approach of 'little and often' with writing can be effective. We look for opportunities in every area, for example writing a shopping list in the home corner or labelling models in the construction area.

Writing for a purpose is always important for any child but there are four main points to consider:

Reason – why are you doing it?
Audience – who is it for?
Features – what to put in it, e.g. make sure it is phonetically plausible
Tone – type of writing, e.g. instructions, a letter, poster, fact file, or a card.

My biggest top tip for supporting writing in Early Years is to create a vertical writing surface and gross motor writing opportunities too.

It is crucial for children to develop a life-long love of reading. Reading consists of two dimensions: language comprehension and word reading. Language comprehension (necessary for both reading and writing) starts from birth. It only develops when adults talk with children about the world around them and the books (stories and non-fiction) they read with them, and enjoy rhymes, poems and songs together. Skilled word reading, taught later, involves both the speedy working out of the pronunciation of unfamiliar printed words (decoding) and the speedy recognition of familiar printed words. Writing involves transcription (spelling and handwriting) and composition (articulating ideas and structuring them in speech, before writing).

(DfE, 2024: 10)

Learning objectives for literacy

The following list of learning objectives is from *Development Matters* (DfE, 2023a: 81–83):

- Re-read books to build up their confidence in word reading, their fluency and their understanding and enjoyment

- Read individual letters by saying the sounds for them

- Blend sounds into words, so that they can read short words made up of known letter–sound correspondences

- Read some letter groups that each represent one sound and say sounds for them

- Read a few common exception words matched to the school's phonic programme

- Read simple phrases and sentences made up of words with known letter–sound correspondences and, where necessary, a few exception words

- Form lower-case and capital letters correctly

- Spell words by identifying the sounds and then writing the sound with letter/s

- Write short sentences with words with known letter–sound correspondences using a capital letter and full stop

- Re-read what they have written to check that it makes sense.

Early Learning Goals for literacy

ELG: Comprehension

The following list is developed from *Early Years Foundation Stage Profile: 2024 handbook* (DfE 2023b: Annex A: 25–26):

- Demonstrate understanding of what has been read to them by retelling stories and narratives using their own words and recently introduced vocabulary

- Anticipate – where appropriate – key events in stories

- Use and understand recently introduced vocabulary during discussions about stories, non-fiction, rhymes and poems and during role-play.

ELG: Word Reading

- Say a sound for each letter in the alphabet and at least 10 digraphs

- Read words consistent with their phonic knowledge by sound-blending

- Read aloud simple sentences and books that are consistent with their phonic knowledge, including some common exception words.

ELG: Writing

- Write recognisable letters, most of which are correctly formed

- Spell words by identifying sounds in them and representing the sounds with a letter or letters

- Write simple phrases and sentences that can be read by others.

Capital letter match

Learning objective: Form lower-case and capital letters correctly

ELGs: Word Reading, Writing

Resources you will need

- Magnetic letters.

Step-by-step instructions

Activity 1

- Use a chalk pen and write the lower-case letters on the table or tuff tray
- Instruct the children to match the magnetic capital letters with the lower-case letters.

This learning activity can be achieved both ways around; lower-case to capital and capital to lower-case.

Activity 2

- Split the table or tray into two with labels of 'Lower-case' and 'Capital' letters
- Spread the magnetic letters out onto the area
- Ask the children, 'Can you sort out the magnetic letters? Which ones are lower-case? Which ones are capital letters?'

Key vocabulary and questions

- Lower-case letter
- Capital letter
- Small/big
- Sound/letter
- Match.

Adaptations which can be made

- The activity can easily be adapted for younger children by using the letters in their name

- Start with a small amount of letters to match first

- Want to extend this activity? Children can write the matching lower-case and capital letter. This can be done in a variety of ways including chalk, water paint, painting, on a whiteboard, light-up boards and more.

Figure 4.1   A tray of capital letters waiting to be united with their lower-case counterparts

Pre-writing pocket dice

Learning objective: Form lower-case and capital letters correctly
ELG: Writing

Resources you will need

- Pocket dice
- Paper and pencil

Step-by-step instructions

- Draw dots on either side of the paper
- Draw pre-writing patterns on small pieces of paper and stick them onto the pocket dice
- Roll the dice and instruct the children to copy the pattern from one dot along the page to the other side.

Key vocabulary and questions

- Copy
- Left/right
- Start/end
- Roll.

Adaptations which can be made

- Add some gross motor skills practise to this activity by rolling the dice and copying the pattern on a large scale, such as using chalk or a paint brush on the end of a hockey stick to paint the pattern.

Figure 4.2   Using pocket dice to practise copying patterns

Sensory letters

Resources you will need

- Rice
- Lentils
- Sand
- Glitter
- Salt
- Sequins
- Shaving foam.

Step-by-step instructions

- Pour the sensory resource onto a tray
- Encourage the children to explore sensory play. Ask them what they can feel. Can they mark make in it? What letters can they make? Ask them, 'Can you write ____?' or, 'I can draw a picture of me, can you?'

Key vocabulary and questions

- Sound/letter
- Number names.

Adaptations which can be made

The focus of this activity if writing letters would be the formation of them in line with your phonics scheme and rhymes they use.

Figure 4.3   Letters can be traced into lentils, as well as rice, glitter, or any similar resource you have to hand

Figure 4.4   Letters can be traced in glitter using the end of paint brushes

Sentence writing

Learning objectives: Write short sentences with words with known letter-sound correspondences using a capital letter and full stop; Re-read what they have written to check that it makes sense
ELG: Writing

Resources you will need

- Access to the internet
- An interactive whiteboard.

Step-by-step instructions

Activity 1

- A great way to encourage children to write sentences is to use visuals
- Using 'I spy' pictures helps to create great sentences, first orally and then written
- For example: 'I can see a cat', 'I can see a tent', 'I can see a frog and a ship.'

Activity 2

- Once Upon A Picture is a fabulous website FULL of visuals (www.onceuponapicture.co.uk).
- Use these to build sentences on
- You can also use the questions provided on this website to ask children about the images.

Activity 3

- 'Busy picture' images are another great visual tool on which to build sentences, either orally or for writing.

Key vocabulary and questions

- What can you see?

Adaptations which can be made

Build and expand upon the child's sentence, e.g. 'I can see a car', to, for example, 'I can see a big red car'.

Figure 4.5 Using 'I spy' pictures to help children create sentences

Blending game

Learning objective: Blend sounds into words, so that they can read short words made up of known letter–sound correspondences

ELG: Word Reading

Resources you will need

- Hoops
- Playdough
- Paper plates
- Music.

Step-by-step instructions

Activity 1 – What's in the fridge?

- Pretend to open up the fridge and take a peek inside
- Say, 'I can see a ....'
- Segment the word, and see if the children can blend the word together
- Use words which are a mixture between real things you would find in the fridge and funny things (These always go down well with the children!)
- I always ensure the words I say are objects you can pick up, e.g. 'ham' or 'mud', rather than adjectives or conceptual words, such as 'red' or 'space'.

Activity 2 – Hoop jump

- Place the correct amount of hoops in a line on the floor (one hoop per sound)
- Pick a word and sound it out, e.g. 'fox'
- Every time you step/jump into a hoop, say the next sound, e.g. 'f-o-x'.

Activity 3 – Playdough push

- Write a word down on a piece of paper, e.g. 'van'
- Roll a piece of playdough into a ball for each sound
- As you push the playdough down, say the sound.

Activity 4 – Musical reading

- Write a different CVC word on each paper plate and lay them down into a circle

- A little like musical bumps or chairs, when the music stops, a child takes a plate and reads the word

- This could be adapted to numbers, tricky words and more!

Figure 4.6   Mixing physical activity with blending sounds into words

Figure 4.7   'Musical reading' is a fun and adaptable activity

Figure 4.8   Each button represents a sound

Figure 4.9   Children press the 'sound buttons' to help them read the words in this activity

What's in the box?

Learning objectives: Form lower-case and capital letters correctly; Spell words by identifying the sounds and then writing the sound with letter/s
ELG: Writing

Resources you will need

- A box or tray
- CVC word items you have around your classroom (or in line with where the children's phonics learning is).

Step-by-step instructions

- Put all the items into a box or tray
- Ask the children, 'What can you see in the box?'
- The children write a list of what they can see.

Key vocabulary and questions

- For example, dog, cat, bag, mat, sad, mad, web, van, mug, cup, map, jam, hat, fan, peg, pen, pig, hen, mud, leg, rat, vet, link, lamp, crab, hand, tent, flag, frog, plug, stick, chick.

Figure 4.10   The 'What's in the box?' activity is a great opportunity for children to develop spelling skills

Read it, make it, write it

Learning objectives: Read a few common exception words matched to the school's phonic programme; Read simple phrases and sentences made up of words with known letter–sound correspondences and, where necessary, a few exception words; Form lower-case and capital letters correctly; Spell words by identifying the sounds and then writing the sound with letter/s
ELGs: Word Reading; Writing

Resources you will need

- Whiteboard
- Whiteboard pen
- Magnetic letters
- Images of CVC, CVCC, and CCVC word items.

Step-by-step instructions

- Use the whiteboard pen to split the board into three sections labelled: Read it, Make it, Write it
- The child picks a picture and places it in the top section
- They say what the picture is
- Then they make the word using the magnetic letters in the middle section
- Finally, they write the word in the bottom section.

Key vocabulary and questions

- Letter names/sounds
- Letter formation rhymes.

Adaptations which can be made

This activity can also be adapted for numbers too. Say the number, make the number in different ways and then write the number.

Figure 4.11   This activity works with a child's name, or any number of different words

I spy list

Learning objectives: Form lower-case and capital letters correctly; Spell words by identifying the sounds and then writing the sound with letter/s
ELG: Writing

Resources you will need

- Print off 'I spy' sheets from Google Images
- Whiteboard and whiteboard pen.

Step-by-step instructions

Ask the children:

- 'What pictures can you see?'
- 'Can you write a list of what you can see?'

Adaptations which can be made

- The pictures you can use will depend on where your children are within the phonics scheme. Please ensure you only provide pictures which include sounds the children would be able to write
- 'I spy' can be played verbally to encourage blending. For example, 'I spy with my little eye … b-a-g. What can I see?'

Figure 4.12   As well as 'I spy' sheets, why not try using a bottle filled with surprise objects and rice to hide them from view?

Letter mix-up

Learning objective: Blend sounds into words, so that they can read short words made up of known letter-sound correspondences

ELG: Word Reading

Resources you will need

- Pictures of CVC/CVCC/CCVC words items
- Paper
- Marker
- Sticky-back plastic (optional).

Step-by-step instructions

- Use the sticky-back plastic to stick the pictures to the table
- Write the letters/sounds for each picture on pieces of paper and then mix up the order
- Ask the children to un-jumble the letters/sounds to make the word.

Key vocabulary and questions

- Letter names/sounds
- What sound comes next?
- Can you point to the sounds and read the word?

Adaptations which can be made

This will depend on the phonics scheme and the time of year you complete this activity – ensure you only use the sounds the children know.

Figure 4.13 Using sounds the children have learnt recently will help to consolidate their learning

DIY scratch cards

Learning objectives: Read individual letters by saying the sounds for them; Blend sounds into words, so that they can read short words made up of known letter-sound correspondences; Read some letter groups that each represent one sound and say sounds for them; Read a few common exception words matched to the school's phonic programme
ELG: Word Reading

Resources you will need

- Cardboard
- Sellotape
- PVA glue
- Acrylic paint
- 2p coins
- Black marker.

Step-by step-instructions

- Write a word onto the cardboard
- Use the Sellotape to cover over the whole piece of cardboard
- Mix together the acrylic paint and glue and spread it across the word (this may need two coats of paint)
- Let it dry
- The children use the coin to scratch off the paint and reveal the word.

Key vocabulary and questions

- Letter names/sounds.

Adaptations which can be made

This activity can be adapted for single sounds or words as well as missing letters.

Figure 4.14   What word will be revealed today?

5.
Mathematics

Mathematical development is split into two sub-sections; number and numeral patterns. Not so simply, the children need to develop a wide and varied concept of numbers and links between them. Maths is my all-time favourite! Although just because a child can count to 100, it does not mean they are great at maths. It's more than this. It's number sense, representations, exploring weight, length and capacity and so much more. Maths in reception is all about giving children the foundations of mathematical knowledge and language to support them and make links as they learn more. Although there are schemes of maths to follow if needed, we do not follow a scheme.

Children must be able to feel maths in their hands before they understand it. Maths in reception should be full of hands-on learning with concrete objects before moving to pictorial and abstract concepts (the CPA approach).

Maths is everywhere! Maths doesn't have to be just inside a classroom. And who doesn't love Numberblocks!

Again, this area of learning is not a prime area, but children do need to achieve the early learning goal to reach a good level of development.

Developing a strong grounding in numbers is essential so that all children develop the necessary building blocks to excel mathematically. Children should be able to count confidently, develop a deep understanding of the numbers to 10, the relationships between them and the patterns within those numbers. By providing frequent and varied opportunities to build and apply this understanding – such as using manipulatives, including small pebbles and tens frames for organising counting – children will develop a secure base of knowledge and vocabulary from which mastery of mathematics is built. In addition, it is important that the curriculum includes rich opportunities for children to develop their spatial reasoning skills across all areas of mathematics including shape, space and measures. It is important that children develop positive attitudes and interests in mathematics, look for patterns and relationships, spot connections, 'have a go', talk to adults and peers about what they notice and not be afraid to make mistakes.

(DfE, 2024: 10)

Learning objectives for mathematics

The following list of learning objectives is from *Development Matters* (DfE, 2023a: 93–98):

- Count objects, actions and sounds
- Subitise
- Link the number symbol (numeral) with its cardinal number value
- Understand the 'one more than/one less than' relationship between consecutive numbers
- Explore the composition of numbers to 10
- Automatically recall number bonds for numbers 0–5 and some to 10
- Count beyond ten
- Compare numbers
- Select, rotate and manipulate shapes in order to develop spatial reasoning skills
- Compose and decompose shapes so that children recognise a shape can have other shapes within it, just as numbers can
- Continue, copy and create repeating patterns
- Compare length, weight and capacity

Early Learning Goals for mathematics

ELG: Number

The following list is developed from *Early Years Foundation Stage Profile: 2024 handbook* (DfE 2023b: Annex A: 246–27):

- Have a deep understanding of number to 10, including the composition of each number

- Subitise (recognise quantities without counting) up to 5

- Automatically recall (without reference to rhymes, counting or other aids) number bonds up to 5 (including subtraction facts) and some number bonds to 10, including double facts.

ELG: Numerical Patterns

- Verbally count beyond 20, recognising the pattern of the counting system

- Compare quantities up to 10 in different contexts, recognising when one quantity is greater than, less than or the same as the other quantity

- Explore and represent patterns within numbers up to 10, including evens and odds, double facts and how quantities can be distributed equally.

Counting stones

Learning objectives: Count objects, actions and sounds; Link the number symbol (numeral) with its cardinal number value; Count beyond ten
ELG: Number

Resources you will need

- Metal tin (Ikea sell a small metal plant pot for 50p which is great)
- Small pebbles or glass gems. Glass gems are always a winner because they entice the children's interest. You can also get so many different colours. These also make for great loose parts within your classroom.

Step-by-step instructions

- Model counting to 10 before the activity starts, with everyone joining in
- Say, 'Now let's listen carefully to see how many we can hear'
- Drop one pebble or gem at a time into the metal tin and model (with the children) counting one number as one gem is dropped
- Ask, 'How many do we have altogether? What is our final number?'
- Once you have a certain number in the tin, empty out the gems on the carpet or table and count them out loud to check the final number
- This activity can then be added into provision for the children to play independently.

Key vocabulary and questions

- Listening carefully
- Count/counting
- Numerals (depending on the amount you are counting up to)
- Can you listen carefully and see how many gems you can hear drop into the tin?
- Was it 5 or 7?
- Count along with me: 1, 2, 3 …

- Remember, count one number for one drop
- How many do we have altogether?
- What is our final number?

Adaptations which can be made

- Change the numerals you are using
- Ensure the resources are large enough that they cannot be mouthed or swallowed.

Figure 5.1   The counting stones activity can be added into provision for independent play

1:1 correspondence

Learning objectives: Count objects, actions and sounds; Link the number symbol (numeral) with its cardinal number value; Count beyond ten

ELG: Number

Resources you will need

- Sorting objects
- Numeral cards.

Step-by-step instructions

- Lay out the number cards and objects onto a table
- A child picks a number card and counts out the correct amount
- Use the objects to help the children practise counting, for example ask a child to pick out a certain number of different objects, or a certain number of objects with a particular characteristic, e.g. colour or shape.

Key vocabulary and questions

- Count/counting
- How many?
- What number is this?
- Can you count five red objects?
- Can you count seven different objects?
- Can you count three objects with wheels?

Figure 5.2 Using colourful objects can add extra fun to counting

Sensory number writing

Learning objective: Count beyond ten
ELG: Number

Activity 1 - Number rhymes

Learning to write numbers can be tricky but I like to use a rhyme to help support the formation.

- Zero starts the show. Just a circle all alone, you know. Straight down, then around, that's how you go. To make a zero, nice and round, not too slow!

- One is simple, just a stick. Straight and tall, not too quick. Down we go, then we're done. One straight line, that's how it's spun

- Two's a curve that's oh so neat. Around and back, it's quite a treat. A curvy path from top to bottom. Two little loops, we've got 'em!

- Three's a curve with a twist. Around, down, then back like this. A loop, a line, then you're done. Three's ready to join the fun!

- Four's a square, just go down, then right. Across the top, then down the side, that's right. A line across, and down some more. Four sides make a shape to adore

- Five's a number with a hook. Down, around, and back we look. A line across, a curl so bright. Five's formation is just right

- Six is like a big balloon. Round and round, then a loop's in tune. A curve, a line, and you're set. Six's formation, don't forget!

- Seven's easy, just a line. Straight and tall, that's just fine. A slanting stroke, then across we sail. Seven's formation, a simple tale

- Eight's a pair, a circle's show. Around we go, then back we flow. A curve, a curve, and we can relate. Eight's formation, isn't it great?

- Nine's a loop, a backward sign. Around, down, then a line to find. A curl, a line, and you're through. Nine's formation, this is true

- Ten is one and zero's pair, a stick, a circle, that's a fair share. A line, a round, then it's done. Ten's formation, join the fun!

We all know paper and pencils can be good but there's nothing more exciting for some children than multi-sensory tactile learning. So creating hands-on learning experiences where the children can write numbers using various different objects or materials can make these even more enjoyable. These could include:

- Salt
- Flour
- Lentils
- Light-up writing pads
- Dry wipe wallets
- Acrylic boards
- Chalking outside
- Painting
- Gross motor painting
- Using highlighters
- Rainbow numbers
- Water painting onto the floor.

Please ensure an adult is supervising when children are accessing this activity if food is involved.

Other activities to try

Roll the dice and write the number. This is simple but effective, and year-on-year my class loves this idea.

Figure 5.3   Using something like salt can provide children with a sensory experience while they learn to write numbers

Composition of numbers

Learning objective: Explore the composition of numbers to 10
ELG: Number, Numerical Patterns

Resources you will need

- Part part whole model
- Numicon
- Objects or counters
- SumBlox.

Step-by-step instructions

Activity 1 – Using SumBlox

- Ask, 'How can you make a whole number using smaller numbers?'
- Let the children explore the SumBlox. These are wooden blocks which are numerals, but each number is a different size. The numbers get bigger the higher their value. So, if you were to put 2 and 3 on top of each other, this would be the same size as 5, and so on.

Activity 2 – Using a part part whole model

- If my whole number is 8, how can I make two smaller numbers to make 8 in total? Use the counters or objects to explore.

Activity 3 – Using Numicon

- Choose your whole number
- Place the Numicon beads onto each of the holes
- Pick a small piece to place on top. Now how many holes do you have left?
- Pick that number Numicon
- This is similar to the part part whole model, but using Numicon and stacking instead.

Key vocabulary and questions

- Smaller, bigger, larger
- Whole number
- Part part whole model
- What is part of a number?
- What other numbers could I use?

Adaptations which can be made

- Challenge the children by making the same whole number but in different ways, e.g. 8 can be made with 4 and 4 but also with 6 and 2. How else can you make it?
- You could also incorporate weight into this activity using Numicon. For example, if I have 10 this side as my whole number, what other numbers could I put together to make the same amount?

This is why I love Numicon so much as it is weighted and so versatile!

Figure 5.4   Let children explore numbers through play

Number splat

Learning objective: Count objects, actions and sounds
ELG: Number

Resources you will need

- Number cards
- Fly swatter.

Step-by-step instructions

- Place number cards onto a surface
- Say, 'Can you splat the number ... ?'
- The children take it in turns to use the fly swatter to 'splat' the correct number
- If you do not have a fly swatter, this activity can easily be recreated just using your hand.

Once modelled, the children love to play this game independently.

Key vocabulary and questions

- Can you splat number ... ?
- Number names
- Turn-taking
- Who's turn is next?

Adaptations which can be made

- You can adapt this activity by starting off with the numbers in order and then challenging the children further by mixing the numbers up

- Simplify this activity by giving just two number options or recognising the numbers first before the game.

Figure 5.5   Children love to 'splat' the numbers!

One more, one less than

Learning objective: Understand the 'one more than/one less than' relationship between consecutive numbers
ELG: Numerical Patterns

Resources you will need

- Duplo blocks
- Paper and pen
- Whiteboard pen
- Dry wipe wallet
- Optional support: number line.

Step-by-step instructions

- On the paper, draw a grid with three columns and two rows (one small and one large)
- Along the top row write: 'One less', 'My number' and 'One more'
- Place the sheet into the dry wipe wallet (this is so you can re-use the sheet over and over)
- In the middle column, write a number using the whiteboard pen
- Ask, 'Can you use the Duplo to make a tower of one more than my number and one less than my number?'

Key vocabulary and questions

- Does one more make the number bigger or smaller?
- Let's check on the number line/stairs
- Smaller/bigger
- Number names, e.g. four, five, six
- What number is this?

Adaptations which can be made

- If you do not have Duplo, this can be done using different resources too such as counters or sorting objects

- To make this activity easier, add a number line or stairs for the children to use as a visual aid to support their counting of one more or one less.

Figure 5.6   Using a number line or stairs helps children visually in counting one more or one less

Shadow play

Learning objectives: Select, rotate and manipulate shapes in order to develop spatial reasoning skills; Compose and decompose shapes so that children recognise a shape can have other shapes within it, just as numbers can

Resources you will need

- Chalk pen
- 2D shapes
- Tuff tray.

Step-by-step instructions

- Draw around the 2D shapes using the chalk pen
- Ask the children if they can match the 2D shapes with the correct shadow
- Then ask them to identify the name of the shape, and how they knew that it matched.

Key vocabulary and questions

- Shape names (circle, square, triangle, rectangle, star, oval, heart, rhombus)
- Match
- Same/different.

Adaptations which can be made

You can also do this with different objects around the classroom, not just shapes. For example, Numicon, scissors, pencil, paint brush, and building blocks will all give different shadows.

Figure 5.7 As well as cut-out shapes, all kinds of different objects could be used in shadow play

Exploring length, weight and capacity

Learning objective: Compare length, weight and capacity

1. Length
Resources you will need

- Measuring worms
- Multilink cubes
- Playdough
- Objects to measure
- Chalk pen
- Optional: ruler/measuring tape.

Step-by-step instructions

- When learning about length, I always suggest letting the children explore the resources first, before using the thinking out loud technique, for example, 'I wonder which worm is longer'
- Place some objects onto the table and use non-standard units of measure to see how long they are. For example, 'This elephant is five cubes long', 'This elephant is one hand long', 'This elephant is ten sequins long', etc
- Ask the children to make 'sausages' out of playdough
- Ask them which one is the longest, and which one is the shortest
- Say, 'I think I can make one longer than this; let me try'
- Draw some straight lines onto the table using the chalk pen. Ask the children if they can find something in the classroom longer or shorter than this line.

Key vocabulary and questions

- Long, longer, longest
- Short, shorter, shortest

- Order
- Centimetres/inches.

Be clear on the language you use, which is different depending on whether you are measuring length or height.

Adaptations which can be made

Challenge the children to put the objects in order of length from shortest to longest. The fewer the objects, the easier it is.

2.   Weight

Resources you will need

- Balancing scales
- Objects to weigh (at different sizes)
- Numicon.

Step-by-step instructions

When it comes to teaching weight, I believe you should let the children explore the balancing scales first.

- Invite the children, 'Can you explore the objects on the different sides of the scales? What happened?' Think out loud, 'That made the scales go down; that means it is heavy'. Ask, 'What happened to the other side?'
- Explore Numicon with the balancing scales. For example, 'If I have five sides, how many do I need on the other side to make it balanced?'

The following is a good activity aimed at addressing misconceptions of weight:

- Start with a wrapped box with objects inside of various sizes and weights
- Get the children to predict which object is going to be heaviest without holding them (just by sight)
- Then test their predictions using the balancing scales (choose a big box which is light and a small box which is heavy using objects such as a balloon and rice)

- Help the children understand that just because an object is big, it doesn't mean it is heavy, and vice versa.

Key vocabulary and questions

- Heavy, heaviest
- Light, lightest
- Balanced/same.

Adaptations which can be made

- Extend this activity by predicting which object is going to be heavier or lighter, then test out your prediction to see if you were correct
- Challenge the children by asking them to put the objects in order, from lightest to heaviest.

3. Capacity

Resources you will need

- Water tray
- Lentils **(Please ensure the children have adult supervision)**
- Sand
- Different sized containers.

Step-by-step instructions

Before introducing the vocabulary of capacity to the children, I would allow them to explore the resources.

Activity 1

- At snack time, when each child gets their water bottle, you can discuss capacity language, such as, 'My water bottle is half full'.

Activity 2

- Explore capacity using different resources, such as water, sand or lentils. Say, 'Can you make the cup full of water? Can you make the bottle nearly empty?' This is a great opportunity for some hands-on, tactile learning, but just remember that not every child enjoys this.

Activity 3

- Address the misconception of using different sized and shaped containers
- Ask, 'How can we describe how much water is in this bottle using our capacity language?'
- Ask the children what they think will happen if you pour the same amount into a differently shaped bottle, e.g. long and skinny
- Ask them to predict, then test it
- Take another differently shaped bottle, for example wide and short, and repeat.

Key vocabulary and questions

- Full
- Empty
- Half full, half empty
- Nearly full
- Nearly empty.

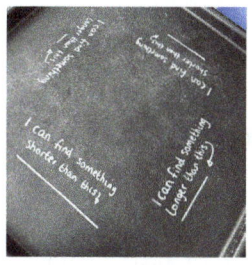

Figure 5.8 Using objects in the children's surroundings to help them learn about different lengths

Figure 5.9 Using non-standard units of measure helps children when they begin to learn about length

Figure 5.10 Let the children explore the balancing scales before introducing an activity

Figure 5.11 Use cups, jugs, and other items to compare the capacity of differently shaped containers

Odd and even numbers

Learning objectives: Explore the composition of numbers to 10; Compare numbers
ELG: Numerical Patterns

Resources you will need

- Numicon
- Feely tub
- Number line
- 100 square.

Step-by-step instructions

- Explain that odd and even numbers are just like a repeating pattern: odd, even, odd, even, odd, even, etc

Activity 1

- Ask the children to colour the numbers in on the number line to represent if they are odd or even.

Activity 2

- Place a piece of Numicon into the feely tub
- Tell the children not to look, then ask them whether they think it is odd or even. Ask them, 'How do you know?'
- The simple way of teaching this is to explain that the even Numicon pieces all have a 'friend' next to them, but the odd ones are by themselves (the sticky out part)
- This is a great game to add into provision for the children to practise this with their friends.

Key vocabulary and questions

- Odd
- Even

- Repeating pattern
- Notice
- Number names, e.g. two, four, six, eight, ten, etc.

Adaptations which can be made

Challenge the children by colouring the odd numbers onto a 100 square. Ask them, 'What do you notice?'

Figure 5.12   Numicon can be used as a visual way of teaching about odd and even numbers

Doubling butterfly

Learning objective: Explore and represent patterns within numbers up to 10, including evens and odds, double facts and how qualities can be distributed
ELGs: Number, Numerical Patterns

Resources you will need

- Chalk pen
- Tuff tray
- Counters.

Step-by-step instructions

- Use the chalk pen to draw a picture of a butterfly or ladybird on the tuff tray and add counters on to some of them
- Write some suggested doubling number sentences with a blank answer for the children to work out
- Explain that we need to have the same amount on both sides
- Ask, 'How many do we have here? So, how many do we need to have on this side?'
- Now we need to work out the answer. Ask them, 'How many are there altogether?'
- Write the answer and read the number sentence, e.g. 3 + 3 = 6.

Key vocabulary and questions

- Double, doubling
- Addition, add, plus
- Equals, makes, altogether.

Figure 5.13   Using outlines of butterflies or ladybirds is ideal for this doubling activity

6.
Understanding the world

Understanding the world is split into three sub-sections: past and present, the natural world, and families and communities. Understanding the world is how children make sense of the world around them. However much it pains me to say, consider it the non-core of the national curriculum: Science, History, Geography and RE (Religious Education).

Children don't need to reach the Early Learning Goals to achieve a good level of development but of course it doesn't mean we're not going to be teaching them. These are usually the typical 'topic' part of learning.

Over the years, I've done topics in many different ways:

- A half-termly topic linked to a story book per week
- A weekly or fortnightly topic
- A termly topic split into subtopics, e.g. animals as the overarching topic, then weeks of animals and their babies, Arctic animals, jungle animals, etc.

It's also so important to get to know the cohort you have and to celebrate what is special about them. It's as important to be open to new children as it is the ones you normally cover. Always ensure everyone is valued in your classroom. This is something we usually discuss during home visits with our parents.

A large part of teaching our understanding of the world is to take a local walk in the autumn term. We can also build in a simple map world, the changes of the season, our weekly welly walks and celebrating British Science Week.

Understanding the world involves guiding children to make sense of their physical world and their community. The frequency and range of children's personal experiences increases their knowledge and sense of the world around them – from visiting parks, libraries and museums to meeting important members of society such as police officers, nurses and firefighters. In addition, listening to a broad selection of stories, non-fiction, rhymes and poems will foster their understanding of our culturally, socially, technologically and ecologically diverse world. As well as building important knowledge, this extends their familiarity with words that support understanding across domains. Enriching and widening children's vocabulary will support later reading comprehension.

(DfE, 2024: 11)

Learning objectives for understanding the world

The following list of learning objectives is from *Development Matters* (DfE, 2023a: 108–113):

- Comment on images of familiar situations in the past
- Compare and contrast characters from stories, including figures from the past
- Recognise some similarities and differences between life in this country and life in other countries
- Talk about members of their immediate family and community
- Name and describe people who are familiar to them
- Understand that some places are special to members of their community
- Recognise that people have different beliefs and celebrate special times in different ways
- Draw information from a simple map
- Explore the natural world around them
- Describe what they see, hear and feel whilst outside
- Recognise some environments that are different to the one in which they live
- Understand the effect of changing seasons on the natural world around them.

Early Learning Goals for understanding the world

ELG: Past and Present

The following list is developed from *Early Years Foundation Stage Profile: 2024 handbook* (DfE, 2023b: Annex A: 27):

- Talk about the lives of the people around them and their roles in society

- Know some similarities and differences between things in the past and now, drawing on their experiences and what has been read in class

- Understand the past through settings, characters and events encountered in books read in class and storytelling.

ELG: People, Culture and Communities

- Describe their immediate environment using knowledge from observation, discussion, stories, non-fiction texts and maps

- Know some similarities and differences between different religious and cultural communities in this country, drawing on their experiences and what has been read in class

- Explain some similarities and differences between life in this country and life in other countries, drawing on knowledge from stories, non-fiction texts and – when appropriate – maps.

ELG: The Natural World

- Explore the natural world around them, making observations and drawing pictures of animals and plants

- Know some similarities and differences between the natural world around them and contrasting environments, drawing on their experiences and what has been read in class

- Understand some important processes and changes in the natural world around them, including the seasons and changing states of matter.

Classroom treasure map

Learning objective: Draw information from a simple map
ELG: The Natural World

Resources you will need

- Treasure (for this you can use anything; I tend to use golden coins)
- A bird's eye view of your classroom or space you are going to use
- A dry wipe wallet.

Step-by-step instructions

Before this activity, the children will need to have an understanding of how to use a map. To help with this, look on Google Earth at your local area or print off maps and point out key features of your map.

- Together with the children, make a map of your classroom with the key features on. Ask the children, 'Where is the carpet area? Who can tell me where the creative area is?', for example
- Hide some golden coins somewhere in your classroom and mark on the map with an 'X'
- Get the children to work in partners or groups to work out where to go so they can find the treasure. Ask them, 'How did you work out where to go? Which way?'
- Add in some mathematical learning too, such as hiding ten coins and using a ten frame. Ask, 'How many coins do we have to find? We have found four, now how many do we still need to find?' etc.

Adaptations which can be made

- Take this activity outside or to other areas of your classroom
- The children can make their own map of the classroom and then hide the treasure
- Make an obstacle course in which the children can guide each other around blindfolded.

Making a map is tricky, so if your child is struggling with this, then start by helping them to create their own map such as a treasure map or looking at maps of your local area and pointing out key features which would be recognisable to the child.

Figure 6.1 Using a familiar surrounding can help children to learn about using a map

Figure 6.2 Use simple templates so children can create their own treasure maps

Growing worms

Resources you will need

- Three paper kitchen towel sheets
- Pen
- Washable felt pens
- Permanent marker
- Pipette
- Water
- Plate or bowl.

Step-by-step instructions

I would suggest modelling this activity first then in small groups getting children to have a go themselves.

- Cut a paper towel sheet in half
- Colour one side lightly with washable felt pens
- Roll the paper around a pen to make it look like a worm
- Scrunch each side together and then remove from the pen
- Add eyes and a mouth with a permanent marker if you wish on one end to make a face
- Provide a dish of water and pipette and drop some water onto the worm to make the worm grow and become colourful!

Key vocabulary and questions

- Colour, names of colours
- Droplet, drip, drop, splash
- Scrunch
- Roll, around
- Facial features such as eyes, mouth, etc.

Figure 6.3   The resources you need for this activity: kitchen roll coloured in, pipette, water and a tray

Figure 6.4   Wrap the coloured kitchen roll around a felt pen

Figure 6.5   The coloured worms are in the tray, waiting to grow!

Figure 6.6   Using the pipette to make the worms magically grow!

Floating and sinking

Resources you will need

- A collection of different objects (some of which will float and some of which will sink)
- A plastic bowl
- Water
- Tuff tray
- Chalk pen.

Step-by-step instructions

- Use the chalk pen to divide the tuff tray into 'Sink' and 'Float' categories
- Draw a small box next to each title, marking an 'X' at the bottom for 'Sink' and at the top for 'Float' (so children can visually associate the word with the action)
- Fill the plastic bowl with water
- Place the objects around the plastic bowl and explore placing the objects into the bowl to experiment if they are going to sink or float
- Place the objects into the correct part of the table.

Key vocabulary and questions

- I see .../I wonder .../I notice ...
- Predict
- Observe/watch.

Figure 6.7   Let's see what floats and what sinks

Seasonal play
Autumn – Leaf printing

Learning objective: Understand the effect of changing seasons on the natural world around them
ELG: The Natural World

Resources you will need

- Different sized leaves from different trees
- Paint (autumnal colours)
- Paint brush
- Paper (either pieces per child or done as a whole group collaborative piece).

Step-by-step instructions

Instruct the children to do the following:

- Paint the back of the leaf and place it onto the paper
- Push the leaf down and then peel the leaf away to see the print.

Key vocabulary, questions and adaptations

- Consider using different sized leaves to add in the mathematical language of size
- Suggest to the children that they count the number of leaves they have printed
- Ask, 'What colours are you going to use and why?'
- Suggest that they place the leaves in a way to create a picture
- Look at the book 'Leaf Man' by Lois Ehlert
- These activities could be recreated in the other seasons to compare seasonal colours.

Figure 6.8   Autumnal colours are appropriate for this activity

Winter – Penguin ice skating

Learning objective: Understand the effect of changing seasons on the natural world around them

ELG: The Natural World

Resources you will need

- Small penguin models
- Ice cube tray
- Water
- Freezer.

Step-by-step instructions

- Place the penguins into the ice cube tray, fill with water and place into the freezer to freeze
- Let the children explore them and build upon their language.

Key vocabulary, questions and adaptations

- How did the penguins get stuck in the ice?
- How can we get them out? What should we try? (This is a great opportunity to discuss ice melting, and how we can speed up this process, for example with hammers and salt)
- Use this activity to expand on the children's knowledge of animals and the world around us, e.g. Where do penguins live? Do you know what a baby penguin is called? Use this as an opportunity to increase curiosity about penguins
- Can you slide the penguin along the tray? How far did they go? (This is a little like curling. If it is an Olympic year, instead of penguins, add paper clips to act as curling stones in two colours)
- Create a target on a tuff tray and slide the penguins in ice and see how many points you score. Can you total up your score?

Figure 6.9 Using penguin models can introduce all kinds of interesting topics, such as the melting ice caps

Spring – Life cycles of a frog

Learning objective: Understand the effect of changing seasons on the natural world around them.
ELG: The Natural World

Resources you will need

- Green paper
- Paper
- Pencil/colouring pencils/felt pens.

Step-by-step instructions

This activity should be completed after discussing the lifecycle of a frog.

- Draw or print a picture of a frog onto a piece of green paper
- Cut the frog in half widthways
- Cut a piece of A4 paper in half, then concertina the paper (folding it back and forth) into six parts
- Stick one part of the white piece of paper to the back of half the frog and do the same to the other part. This means as you open up the frog there will be four parts showing and then as you close it the white paper will sit behind the frog picture
- On each of the pieces as you open it up, draw or stick a part of the frog life cycle
- As you open up the frog you will then see the different parts of the life cycle such as:
    - Frog spawn, tadpole, froglet, frog.

Key vocabulary and questions

- How does the life of a frog start? What comes next?
- Have you seen a frog spawn before? Where was it? Where do they live?
- This could be a great chance to talk about the habitats of animals.

Figure 6.10   The life cycle of a frog is a great way to start discussions about the habitats of different animals

Summer – Small world beach

Learning objective: Understand the effect of changing seasons on the natural world around them
ELG: The Natural World

Resources you will need

- Sand
- Water
- Solar water pump
- Boats
- Small models of underwater animals
- Small world people/peg people
- Cocktail umbrellas.

Step-by-step instructions

- Create a beach set up and simply let the children explore!

Key vocabulary and questions

- Have you been to the beach before? What did you see there? What did the sand feel like? Do you like dry or wet sand?
- This is an opportunity to add rubbish to the 'water' to discuss recycling.

Figure 6.11 Some children might never have been to a beach before, so they will have fun exploring!

Shaving foam ice cream shop

Learning objective: Understand the effect of changing seasons on the natural world around them
ELG: The Natural World

Resources you will need

- Shaving foam
- Spoons/ice cream scoops
- Sprinkles
- Squeezy bottles containing coloured water
- Paint
- Stirrers
- Ice cream cones
- Bowls.

Please ensure an adult is supervising when children are participating in this activity, with pretend food involved.

Step-by-step instructions

- Let the children explore the materials, making 'ice cream', adding sprinkles and sauces, and so on
- Ask them, 'I wonder what flavour it's going to be'
- Prompt them to think about when they have ice cream
- Place an ice cream order, e.g. 'Can I have one scoop of strawberry ice cream with rainbow sprinkles please?'

Figure 6.12   Shaving foam makes a good imitation of ice cream ... just make sure the children don't eat it!

Is it magnetic?

Resources you will need

- A collection of objects, both magnetic and not magnetic
- Magnetic wands
- Tuff tray or table
- Chalk pen.

Step-by-step instructions

- Draw a line down the middle on the tuff tray and write a title at the top of each column: 'Magnetic' and 'Not magnetic'
- Place the objects at the bottom of the tray with the magnetic wands
- Use the magnetic wands to explore the objects
- Get the children to explore whether each item is magnetic. Help them to understand the concepts by asking, 'Does it "stick" (attract) to the object? Or does it "push away" (repel) from the object?'

Key vocabulary and questions

- Attract
- Repel.

Figure 6.13   Find a wide variety of objects and magnets to predict and test

Gardening ideas

Learning objectives: Explore the natural world around them; Describe what they see, hear and feel whilst outside; Understand the effect of changing seasons on the natural world around them
ELG: The Natural World

As an increasing number of children grow up in homes without access to gardens, it becomes crucial for educational settings to provide opportunities for children to engage in gardening activities and reap their numerous benefits.

Why gardening?

Gardening presents a wealth of enjoyable and educational opportunities for children, teaching them essential lessons such as plant identification, understanding plant needs for survival, recognising seasonal changes and comprehending the impact of weather on plants.

Benefits of gardening with children in relation to the Early Years Foundation Stage (EYFS):

- Personal, Social and Emotional Development: gardening fosters a sense of responsibility as children care for plants, no matter how small, boosting their confidence and self-esteem. Patience is also nurtured through the gradual growth of plants, encouraging children to appreciate the wonders of nature. Growing vegetables provides a platform for discussing healthy eating habits and trying new foods

- Physical Development: gardening engages children in a variety of motor skills, including using trowels and forks for digging, raking, patting soil, planting, and watering with a watering can

- Communication and Language: gardening activities offer opportunities for enriching language development, introducing children to new vocabulary related to plant names and flower parts, thus promoting linguistic growth

- Mathematics: activities inherently involve mathematical concepts such as counting (e.g. counting seeds or plants), measurement, and understanding capacity

- Understanding the World: participation in planting and nurturing seeds and bulbs allows children to observe nature first hand, gaining insights into the requirements for plant growth and the effects of weather on plants.

What to grow when?

September/October:

- Bulbs: to add some colour to your garden during winter and early spring, consider planting snowdrops, crocus, cyclamen, and daffodils. Once planted, these bulbs require minimal maintenance

- Young plants: now is a suitable time to purchase pansies, violas, and primulas, as they will continue to bloom well into the winter months

- Edible crops: for quick results, plant fast-growing crops such as radishes (mature in six weeks), small varieties of carrots like Parmex, various salad leaves, late-sowing spinach, and salad onions. Note that root vegetables like carrots should be planted directly where they'll grow since they can't be transplanted

- Herbs: if you're looking to introduce herbs to a new plot, consider purchasing established lavender, rosemary, curry plant, and creeping lemon thyme. These evergreen herbs provide aromatic benefits even through winter, with lavender flowers emitting fragrance as they fade

- All these can be cultivated in containers for those without garden space, and many can thrive indoors with regular trimming. Ensure adequate drainage in pots by adding gravel, bark, or even old tea bags to the compost.

November/December:

- Although autumns have been relatively warm lately, refrain from planting outdoors during frost, which can damage roots. Utilise this time for gardening area maintenance, exploring gardening tools, and planning for the next year's seeds

- Capture gardening experiences throughout the year with photographs to foster interest and excitement. Consider incorporating other outdoor learning activities like bug houses and bird feeders

- Indoors, engage in fun activities such as growing kitchen foods like avocado, carrot tops, onions, apple and orange pips. Experiment with growing vegetables in innovative ways, like suspending carrots to observe leaf growth. Use this period for garden planning to optimise space and resources.

January/February:

- Observe the first burst of colour in the garden as bulbs start to emerge, depending on winter conditions. Pansies, primulas, crocuses, snowdrops, and cyclamen should be visible. Start purchasing seeds for the upcoming growing season, with early February suitable for sowing broad beans and other early vegetables. Consider indoor or greenhouse cultivation for an early start.

March/April:

- For edible crops, timing is crucial considering the Easter holidays. Plan planting to ensure seedlings are visible before the break or postponed until after. Succession planting of carrots and onions is recommended, along with introducing tomatoes, beans, peas, cucumbers, and courgettes. Flowers like sweet peas and nasturtiums can also be planted for seasonal bloom
- Herbs like mint, sage, thyme, basil, and coriander are ideal for sowing at this time, offering aromatic benefits and culinary uses. Quick-growing varieties of carrots, salad crops, spring onions, or radishes can still be grown for harvest within weeks.

May:

- Transplant seedlings outdoors, taking precautions against late frosts by protecting tender plants with fleece or cloches. Combat slugs and snails with organic methods like harsh grit or companion planting with comfrey. Monitor progress and evaluate successes and failures for future improvements.

June/July:

- Enjoy the fruits of gardening labour with produce like tomatoes, carrots, spring onions, and salad leaves. Observe flowers in bloom and plan for a prolonged flowering period into autumn. Encourage children's involvement in watering routines, ensuring watering is done during cooler parts of the day to avoid scorching leaves.

August:

- Leave the garden to nature's care for six weeks, hoping for favourable weather conditions.

September (again):

- As the second season approaches, continue to enjoy the remaining harvest of potatoes, onions, and tomatoes. Spring-planted flowers and herbs will continue to flourish. Take the time to tidy up the garden, removing any dead plants and managing weeds

- Ultimately, whether your gardening efforts yield success or not, the key is to inspire children's love for plants and nurture their desire to care for and grow their own.

Figure 6.14   These sunflower shoots will grow to a height of two metres or more!

Figure 6.15   What's growing in the grow bag?

7.
Expressive arts and design

Expressive arts and design is split into two sub-sections: creating with materials, and being imaginative and expressive. Put simply, expressive arts and design is how children express themselves creatively. As with Understanding the world, it pains me to say that this is considered the non-core of the national curriculum: Art, Music and Design Technology.

Creative development in Early Years is all about sparking imagination and demonstrating ways children can use techniques to explore. To me personally, this is a mixture of the process and sometimes the product.

Process = focuses on the process of creating rather than the outcome. It is child directed and celebrates the discovery of exploring.

Product = to achieve the desired effect, for example, if the activity was painting daffodils, you may only have the correct colours out for the children to use.

There is no right or wrong answer in my opinion. I believe you need a mixture of them both; to some, a blank piece of paper could be completely overwhelming, but to others it could be a chance to express themselves.

A consistent junk modelling area within the classroom allows the children to explore, develop their ideas and reflect on their learning. Talking through the process and considering ways of improving it is one of the biggest parts of expressive arts and design learning.

The development of children's artistic and cultural awareness supports their imagination and creativity. It is important that children have regular opportunities to engage with the arts, enabling them to explore and play with a wide range of media and materials. The quality and variety of what children see, hear and participate in is crucial for developing their understanding, self-expression, vocabulary and ability to communicate through the arts. The frequency, repetition and depth of their experiences are fundamental to their progress in interpreting and appreciating what they hear, respond to and observe (DfE 2024: 11).

Learning objectives for expressive arts and design

The following list of learning objectives is from *Development Matters* (DfE, 2023a: 123–126):

- Explore, use and refine a variety of artistic effects to express their ideas and feelings

- Return to and build on their previous learning, refining ideas and developing their ability to represent them

- Create collaboratively, sharing ideas, resources and skills

- Listen attentively, move to and talk about music, expressing their feelings and responses

- Watch and talk about dance and performance art, expressing their feelings and responses

- Sing in a group or on their own, increasingly matching the pitch and following the melody

- Develop storylines in their pretend play

- Explore and engage in music making and dance, performing solo or in groups.

Early Learning Goals for expressive arts and design

ELG: Creating with Materials

The following list is developed from *Early Years Foundation Stage Profile: 2024 handbook* (DfE, 2023b: Annex A: 28).

- Safely use and explore a variety of materials, tools and techniques, experimenting with colour, design, texture, form and function
- Share their creations, explaining the process they have used
- Make use of props and materials when role playing characters in narratives and stories.

ELG: Being Imaginative and Expressive

- Invent, adapt and recount narratives and stories with peers and their teacher
- Sing a range of well-known nursery rhymes and songs
- Perform songs, rhymes, poems and stories with others, and – when appropriate – try to move in time with music.

Exploring colour

Learning objective: Explore, use and refine a variety of artistic effects to express their ideas and feelings
ELG: Creating with Materials

Resources you will need

- Tuff tray
- Chalk pen
- Paint
- Paint brush.

Step-by-step instructions

- Draw a grid onto the tuff tray using the chalk pen
- Draw a key for the different colours of paint at the bottom, e.g.: 1 = red, 2 = yellow, 3 = blue, 4 = pink, 5 = orange, 6 = white, 7 = green, 8 = purple, 9 = brown, 10 = black
- Ask the children if they can recognise the number and paint the square the correct colour by using the key.

Key vocabulary and questions

- Names of colours, e.g. red, blue, green, etc
- Number names, e.g. one, two, three, etc
- Square
- Paint, brush, in the line.

Adaptations which can be made

- This activity can easily be recreated on paper with fewer colours or by using colouring pencils
- Add just the three primary colours on some trays so the children can mix their own secondary colours to use.

Figure 7.1 Using a key is a good way to get children learning about colours

Mixing colours

Learning objectives: Explore, use and refine a variety of artistic effects to express their ideas and feelings; Return to and build on their previous learning, refining ideas and developing their ability to represent them; Create collaboratively, sharing ideas, resources and skills

ELG: Creating with Materials

Resources you will need

- Paint
- Paint brushes
- Paper.

Step-by-step instructions

This activity needs to be modelled first before letting the children explore and complete it independently.

- Using the paint brush, paint one of your hands one of the primary colours, e.g. red
- Paint the other hand a different primary colour, e.g. yellow
- Push your hands together and mix them around
- Ask the children what colour it made (e.g. orange)
- Explore this on a piece of paper by creating a handprint of the first colour (e.g. red), a handprint of the other colour (e.g. yellow) and a handprint at the end (e.g. orange)
- Wash your hands and repeat using the other colours.

Key vocabulary and questions

- Names of colours, e.g. red, yellow, blue
- Primary colours (red, yellow, blue)
- Secondary colours (orange, green, purple)

- Red + yellow = orange
- Blue + red = purple
- Yellow + blue = green.

Adaptations which can be made

- If a child doesn't like the feeling of paint on their hands, then you can squirt the paint into a ziplock bag and mix the colours that way instead
- If your child is struggling with mixing colours, try linking it to a song or using a bar model to suggest how much of a colour they should use.

Figure 7.2   Using paint to learn about mixing colours

Mirror portraits

Learning objectives: Explore, use and refine a variety of artistic effects to express their ideas and feelings; Return to and build on their previous learning, refining ideas and developing their ability to represent them; Create collaboratively, sharing ideas, resources and skills
ELG: Creating with Materials

Resources you will need

- Dry wipe wallet or acrylic board
- Whiteboard pen.

Step-by-step instructions

This is a great activity for partnership work.

- One child holds the dry wipe wallet up to their face, being careful to keep it still
- With the whiteboard pen, the other child draws around their faces, eyes, mouth, hair, etc
- Ask the children, 'Does it look like them? Or does it look funny?'
- Extend this activity by adding on extras, such as a hat or glasses, etc.

Key vocabulary and questions

- Facial features, e.g. eyes, nose, mouth, eyebrows, lips
- What shape is their head?

Adaptations which can be made

• Print off pictures of the children and cut them in half. Stick them to a piece of paper. Ask them to draw the rest of their face. Use wipe off mirrors to draw directly onto to add a new enhancement to the activity.

If your child is struggling with pencil grip and drawing features, then go back to practising fine motor skills.

Figure 7.3   Drawing onto a mirror is a great introduction for children to create their self portrait

Artist – Jackson Pollock

Learning objectives: Explore, use and refine a variety of artistic effects to express their ideas and feelings; Return to and build on their previous learning, refining ideas and developing their ability to represent them; Create collaboratively, sharing ideas, resources and skills
ELG: Creating with Materials

Resources you will need

- Large backing paper or sugar paper
- Paint
- Paint pots.

Step-by-step instructions

When looking at an artist's work, I would recommend firstly explaining what an artist is. You can explain that an artist is someone who creates pictures, such as drawings, paintings, or sculptures. Explain that we can all be artists. Say, 'I am an artist'.

- Explain to the children that you are going to look at an artist called Jackson Pollock and a piece of art he created. You could share a picture of him
- Show the children the piece of art by Jackson Pollock; discuss the colours and how they could recreate this piece of art
- Help the children to think about how the piece of art was created. Suggest, 'Do you think he used felt pens or paint? Do you think he did brush strokes or splattered the paint? How do you think we can move our arms/hands to recreate this effect? Softly or quickly?'
- Mix some paint with a small amount of water into a paint pot (this is to make the paint thinner)
- Lay out the backing paper and let the children paint next to each other
- The 'splatter' technique could be used to replicate the work of Jackson Pollock.

Figure 7.4   Using a 'spatter' technique allows children to create artwork similar in style to Jackson Pollock

Artist – Yayoi Kusama

Learning objectives: Explore, use and refine a variety of artistic effects to express their ideas and feelings; Return to and build on their previous learning, refining ideas and developing their ability to represent them; Create collaboratively, sharing ideas, resources and skills
ELG: Creating with Materials

Resources you will need

- Paper
- Dot stickers.

Step-by-step instructions

When looking at an artist's work, I would recommend firstly explaining what an artist is. You can explain that an artist is someone who creates pictures, such as drawings, paintings, or sculptures. Explain that we can all be artists. Say, 'I am an artist'.

- Explain that you are going to look at an artist called Yayoi Kusama and a piece of art that she created. You could share a picture of Yayoi Kusama

- Explain that this artist creates artwork around polka dots and show the children the piece of art

- Discuss the colours in the artwork and how the children could recreate it. Help them to think about what they could use and their ideas

- Suggest that they try and recreate Yayoi Kusama's artwork using a mixture of different-sized dot stickers to create a polka dot picture.

Linked book: *Yayoi Kusama Covered Everything in Dots and Wasn't Sorry*, Fausto Gilberti (Phaidon Press, 2020).

Figure 7.5   A piece of art created by a child, inspired by Kusama

Artist – Wassily Kandinsky

Learning objectives: Explore, use and refine a variety of artistic effects to express their ideas and feelings; Return to and build on their previous learning, refining ideas and developing their ability to represent them; Create collaboratively, sharing ideas, resources and skills
ELG: Creating with Materials

Resources you will need

- Felt pens/colour pencils/paint/crayons
- Paper.

Step-by-step instructions

When looking at an artist's work, I would recommend firstly explaining what an artist is. You can explain that an artist is someone who creates pictures, such as drawings, paintings, or sculptures. Explain that we can all be artists. Say, 'I am an artist'.

- Explain that you are going to look at an artist called Wassily Kandinsky and a piece of his work. (You could share a picture of the artist)
- Show the children the piece of artwork by Wassily Kandinsky and ask, 'What can you see? What shapes are there? What colours can you see?'
- Suggest that they think about how to recreate this piece. Ask them what they think they could use to create it and take their ideas
- Give each child a piece of square paper to build a collaborative class piece of art, inspired by Kandinsky's concentric circles
- Model to the children creating one piece of the circle, using different colours as it gets bigger. Eventually, the whole piece of paper should have colour on it
- Let the children decide what they wish to use, e.g. paint, colouring crayons, felt pens, or pencils.

Figure 7.6   Kandinsky's concentric circles are wonderful inspiration for children in creating art with vibrant colours and shapes

Artist – Henri Matisse

Learning objectives: Explore, use and refine a variety of artistic effects to express their ideas and feelings; Return to and build on their previous learning, refining ideas and developing their ability to represent them; Create collaboratively, sharing ideas, resources and skills
ELG: Creating with Materials

Resources you will need

- Different shapes cut from different coloured paper of different sizes
- Coloured paper
- Scissors
- Glue
- Pencil.

Step-by-step instructions

When looking at an artist's work, I would recommend firstly explaining what an artist is. You can explain that an artist is someone who creates pictures, such as drawings, paintings, or sculptures. Explain that we can all be artists. Say, 'I am an artist'.

- Explain that you are going to look at an artist called Henri Matisse and a piece of work that he has created. (You could also share a picture of him)
- Explain that Matisse was an artist famous for creating pictures with lots of colours and shapes in a collage
- Show the children an example of Matisse's work, and discuss the colours and shapes
- Ask the children how they think they could recreate their own piece of art like this. Ask them what they could use and take their ideas
- Lay out the different sizes and shapes (numbers 4 or 5 would be good) and invite the children to pick those they like best
- Instruct them to draw or trace the shapes onto coloured paper, then cut them out

212

- Have them carefully lay out the shapes on the piece of paper until they like the design. Let them know that they can do it any way they like

- When they are happy with the design, the children should stick it on another piece of paper; tell them that this is called a collage

- Help the children to experiment with placement, by asking them, 'How does the effect of the collage change when you layer multiple shapes on top of each other?'

- Explore the children's feelings about the art. Ask them, 'How does Henri Matisse's art make you feel? Happy? Confused? Bored?' Reassure them that there's no right or wrong answer and that whatever they think is exactly right. Ask, 'Can you explain why they make you feel this way?'

- Take this further by asking, 'How would the pictures make you feel if he used really dark colours instead?'

Linked books

Matisse's Magical Trail by Tim Hopgood, illus. Sam Boughton (OUP Oxford, 2019).

Snail trail: In Search of a Modern Masterpiece by Jo Saxton (Lincoln Children's Books, 2014).

Henri's Scissors by Jeanette Winter (Beach Lane Books, 2013).

Figure 7.7   Making a Matisse-inspired collage

Problem solving – Rainbows

Resources you will need

- Rainbow pictures
- Laminator/laminating pouches
- Lollipop sticks
- Glue.

Step-by-step instructions

- Laminate the printed rainbows and cut them out
- Draw around the lollipop sticks at different places on the rainbow
- Cut out these pieces and stick them to the lollipop sticks
- Place them onto the table for the children to explore and work out which piece should go where.

Key vocabulary and questions

- Turn around, the other way, positional language
- Where does this one go?
- I wonder if this one goes this way? Oh no, that's the wrong colour, I need to turn it around … there we go.
- Names of colours, e.g. red, orange, yellow, etc.

Adaptations which can be made

- This can be adapted for different pictures where the whole picture is on lollipop sticks. Ask the children if they know which one comes first? Next? Last? What picture did it make?

Figure 7.8   A puzzle made out of rainbow shapes and lollipop sticks makes for a colourful challenge

Design, make, evaluate

Learning objectives: Explore, use and refine a variety of artistic effects to express their ideas and feelings; Return to and build on their previous learning, refining ideas and developing their ability to represent them; Create collaboratively, sharing ideas, resources and skills
ELG: Creating with Materials

Resources you will need

- Design sheet
- Examples of buildings
- Pencils
- Range of construction kits
- Labels
- Space for models to go once made and displayed or for the children to come back to.

Step-by-step instructions

- Invite the children to design a model that they want to build
- Prompt them to explore this, by asking, 'What construction pieces are you going to use? Lego, K'nex, Mobilo? What are you going to build? A car, a helicopter, fire engine, a bridge?'
- Once they have designed it, invite them to go and make it in the construction area
- Once they have finished, remind them to write a label for their model
- Suggest they tell someone about their model. They could tell them how they built it, about the best part of the model, and whether they think they could do anything to improve it and make it better.

Figure 7.9   Giving children a choice of materials to use helps spark their creativity

Small world play

The small world play area provides children with a space to enact both familiar and imaginative scenarios, tapping into their creativity and memories. Within these miniature landscapes, children can recreate scenes from everyday life, stories, fairy tales, or even scenarios that evoke fear or anxiety. These play scenes often feature realistic figurines of animals, people, and scenery, augmented by open-ended and repurposed objects that enhance children's play and foster creativity. Small world play typically revolves around themed interests such as transportation, outer space, dinosaurs, construction, fairy tales, or farms. There are so many benefits to small world play including:

- Stimulating children's imaginations
- Cultivating their interests
- Encouraging creative thinking and idea generation
- Facilitating discussions and meaningful conversations
- Building knowledge about the world, including people, animals, places, and spaces
- Engaging children in fantasy play.

This type of play offers rich learning experiences that may not appear overtly educational but definitely are. It represents child-directed learning, where learning happens seamlessly within the play context. Small world play empowers children as storytellers and masters of their miniature worlds, enabling them to transport themselves to distant and fantastical lands through their imaginations, aided by quality resources, natural materials, colourful fabrics and found objects.

Small world play encompasses a wide range of settings, from real-life scenarios like homes and urban landscapes to fantastical realms. It serves as a versatile tool for exploring complex emotions, issues, and perspectives, allowing children to navigate and understand the world around them and within them.

One of the advantages of small worlds is their scalability and portability, accommodating various play settings – from compact boxes to expansive trays – and offering endless possibilities for indoor and outdoor play.

Through small world play, children act out scenes from reality or fiction using miniature figures and objects, fostering creativity and imagination. Resources for small world play can include purpose-made toys, everyday items from home or the classroom, and natural or recycled materials. The boundless nature of children's imagination ensures that small world play remains an endlessly fascinating and inexhaustible pursuit.

Benefits of small world play

Small world play also contributes to various developmental domains:

Language skills

Children engage with diverse materials, exploring and expanding their vocabulary through social interactions and imaginative scenarios.

Emotional skills

Children have a safe space to explore and express emotions, gaining insight into their feelings and practising coping strategies.

Personal and social skills

Small world play encourages collaboration, conflict resolution, role-playing, and resource sharing, fostering important social competencies.

Maths skills

Children develop numeracy skills through sorting, counting, and problem-solving within the context of small world play.

Understanding the world

Small world play offers a platform for exploring diverse topics, from everyday life to fantastical realms, fostering curiosity and understanding about the world and its complexities.

Small world play provides a holistic learning experience that nurtures children's growth and development across various domains, laying the foundation for lifelong learning and creativity. Common small world play themes include:

- Dinosaurs
- Jungle
- Polar
- Pirates
- Garden
- Insects

- Fairies
- Fairy gardens
- Unicorns
- Mermaids
- Gnomes
- Construction site

- Beach
- Ocean and sea
- Farm
- Favourite story books, such as *We're Going on a Bear Hunt, Room on the Broom*
- Australia
- European/American woodlands
- Fairy tales.

Figure 7.10 Bugs and minibeasts make up a small world setting to teach children about nature

Figure 7.11 Small world play helps to nurture children's interests, for example in the natural or prehistoric world

Figure 7.12 A construction site is another popular small world setting

Figure 7.13 Small world play can also be set up outside

My final message

As you reach the end of this book exploring the infinite wonders of early childhood education, I want to leave you with a heartfelt message that celebrates the essence of learning through play and just how amazing you are and the work you do. The world of a reception-aged child is magical, vibrant, and filled with endless possibilities that you create daily. Through the pages of this book, we've delved into the seven areas of learning, and I hope you've felt the boundless enthusiasm and curiosity that these little learners have with the pleasure of being part of that.

In the realm of play, every moment is a chance to learn, to discover, and to grow. It's more than just building blocks or water play; it's about fostering creativity, enhancing problem-solving skills, and nurturing emotional intelligence. Play is the language children speak fluently, the medium through which they make sense of the world around them. It is in the midst of their imaginative games, messy art projects, and spontaneous dances that the most profound lessons are learned.

Remember, it's not just about the activities outlined in these pages; it's about the spirit with which you approach them. It's about embracing the giggles, the mess, and the unexpected detours in the journey of learning. It's about understanding that in every game, there is a lesson waiting to be discovered and in every puzzle there is a chance for problem-solving. Through play, children learn the value of teamwork, the joy of discovery, and the resilience to try again when they fail.

As educators, parents, and caregivers, your role in this process is immeasurable. You are the guiding stars, the storytellers, and the playmates who make these experiences unforgettable. Embrace the laughter, celebrate the small victories, and cherish the unique qualities of each child under your care. For in this tapestry of play, you are weaving the foundation of their future.

Thank you for embarking on this journey with me.

Hayley

References

Department for Education (DfE) (2023a) *Development Matters.* Available at: www.gov.uk/government/publications/ development-matters--2

Department for Education (DfE) (2023b) *Early Years Foundation Stage Profile: 2024 handbook.* Available at: www.gov.uk/ government/publications/early-years-foundation-stage-profile- handbook

Department for Education (DfE) (2024) *Early Years Foundation Stage Statutory Framework: For group and school-based providers.* Available at: www.gov.uk/government/publications/ early-years-foundation-stage-framework--2

Donaldson, J. (2012) *Room on the Broom.* Macmillan Children's Books.

Early Years Coalition (2021) *Birth to 5 Matters: Non-statutory guidance for the Early Years Foundation Stage.* Early Education. Available at: https://birthto5matters.org.uk/wp-content/ uploads/2021/04/Birthto5Matters-download.pdf

Ehlert, L. *Leaf Man* (2014). Harcourt Brace and Company.

Gilberti, F., (2020) *Yayoi Kusama Covered Everything in Dots and Wasn't Sorry.* Phaidon Press.

Hopgood, T. (2019) *Matisse's Magical Trail*, illus. Sam Boughton. OUP Oxford.

Inside Out film.

Rosen, M. (1989) *We're Going on a Bear Hunt*. Walker Books.

Saxton, J. (2014) *Snail trail: In Search of a Modern Masterpiece*. Lincoln Children's Books.

UNICEF (1989) *The United Nations Convention on the Rights of the Child*. Available at: https://www.unicef.org.uk/wp-content/uploads/2010/05/UNCRC_PRESS200910web.pdf

Winter, J. (2013) *Henri's Scissors*. Beach Lane Books.

www.ingramcontent.com/pod-product-compliance
Lightning Source LLC
Jackson TN
JSHW062324310126
97517JS00011B/110

Contents

About the authors

Amanda Morris is a Psychology Lecturer at the University of Essex, teaching on the foundation year programme. She is also an Associate Lecturer at the Open University, delivering undergraduate psychology. Amanda is a Senior Fellow of the Higher Education Academy and a qualified teacher. She has been teaching psychology for nearly 20 years across undergraduate to GCSE level and has been a senior examiner for numerous external exam boards. As part of her teaching practice, Amanda has a strong interest in the feedback loop and in scaffolding complex concepts and skills to make these accessible to students. Amanda also conducts research in developmental psychology, specifically on the mechanisms that occur during parent–child interactions.

Tracey Elder is a Senior Lecturer and Staff Tutor at the Open University and has been teaching psychology for over 20 years. She is passionate about helping students from all backgrounds achieve their full potential. Tracey has taught psychology across all undergraduate years and has also taught A-level and IB psychology. She has also written A-level papers and been a Chief Examiner. Tracey is a Senior Fellow of the Higher Education Academy. She is also passionate about research, and her research interests are in two distinct areas. Firstly, she is interested in social identity theory and how this may dictate what we are, or are not, permitted to say about our group and others. Her second separate strand of research is in educational psychology, primarily looking at assessment and student performance. Tracey's research has been published in several peer-reviewed journal articles.